POP BUCHANAN

Credit Repair 2026 with Claude

Fix Your Credit Fast with Claude AI, 609 & 611 Dispute Letters, FICO 10T & VantageScore 4.0, Medical Debt Removal, and Trump Era Credit Reporting Changes for 2026–2027

Here is the disclaimer, clean and strong.

DISCLAIMER

This book is written for educational and informational purposes only. Nothing in this publication constitutes legal advice, financial advice, accounting advice, credit counseling, or professional guidance of any kind. The information provided is general in nature and may not apply to your specific situation.

The authors, publishers, and all affiliated companies and individuals, including POPR Technologies Inc. and InvestAI Publishing, make no representations or warranties regarding the accuracy, completeness, or applicability of any information contained in this book. Credit reporting laws, consumer protection regulations, and federal and state statutes change frequently. Readers are responsible for verifying that any information they act on reflects current law at the time of use.

Nothing in this book creates an attorney-client relationship, a financial advisory relationship, or any professional relationship of any kind between the reader and the authors, publishers, or affiliated companies.

Do-it-yourself credit repair is a legal right granted to every American consumer under the Fair Credit Reporting Act. However, every financial situation is different. If you are experiencing serious financial hardship, significant debt, potential bankruptcy, wage garnishment, active litigation, identity theft, or any complex legal or financial situation, we strongly encourage you to consult a licensed attorney, a certified financial planner, a nonprofit credit counselor, or a qualified professional who can evaluate your specific circumstances and provide advice tailored to your situation.

POPR Technologies Inc., InvestAI Publishing, Federal 609, and all related brands, products, and affiliates assume no liability for any action taken or not taken based on the contents of this book. All results described or implied are not guaranteed. Individual outcomes vary based on circumstances, credit file contents, bureau responses, and factors outside the control of the authors or publishers.

This book is sold and distributed with the understanding that the publisher and authors are not engaged in rendering legal, financial, or other professional services through its contents.

Solid. Covers the company. Covers the platform. Covers the AI tools. Protects against liability on all fronts while still being honest that DIY credit repair is a real and legal option. Ready to go on the copyright page.

First edition

This book was professionally typeset on Reedsy.
Find out more at reedsy.com

Contents

Preface

Why This Book Exists, What It Covers, and How to Use It in a Way That Actually Changes Your Financial Life

Welcome back. Or welcome for the first time. Either way, you are in the right place.

If you read Credit Repair 2026 with ChatGPT, you already know the foundation. You know how the bureaus work, what the FCRA gives you the right to do, how to pull your reports, and why the credit system is designed to be confusing to the people it affects most. That book gave you the framework. This one gives you the tools, the prompts, the real letters, the current intelligence on what changed in 2026, and the platform we built specifically so that none of what you learned stays theoretical.

If this is your first time in this series, welcome. You do not need to have read the first book to get full value from this one. Everything you need to understand what we are doing and why is in these pages. But if you finish this book and want to go deeper on the legal foundation, on how the bureaus make money, on the full history of consumer credit law in America, the first book is waiting for you and it will hit differently after this one.

This book was written in 2026 and it reflects 2026. That specificity is intentional and it matters more than it might seem. Credit reporting rules shifted significantly in the past two years. The medical debt landscape changed in ways that have removed or should have removed billions of dollars in negative entries from consumer files across the country. New scoring models from FICO and VantageScore are evaluating your financial behavior differently than any model that came before them, looking at 24 months of your payment and balance history rather than a single snapshot. The regulatory environment around financial technology lending created new risks for borrowers who are rebuilding and do not yet know what a predatory loan structure looks like dressed up as an opportunity. Legislation passed in early 2026 gave mortgage applicants meaningful protection from the information-sharing practices that previously flooded their inboxes the moment they applied for a home loan. These are not background details. They are the operating environment of your financial life right now and this book covers all of them in specific actionable terms, without political commentary, without editorial framing, and without any agenda beyond giving you accurate information about the rules that govern your credit file today.

We also built something. Federal 609 is the official companion application to this book and to Credit Repair 2026 with ChatGPT. It is a browser-based dispute letter engine that takes the legal framework these books teach and turns it into a four-step process that produces a personalized dispute letter from your specific information. The first letter is free. No account required. No credit card required to start. The platform runs entirely in your browser, stores nothing on any server, and was built by a small company with a specific conviction that the tools to navigate the credit system should not cost more than the system already costs the people who need them most. There is a full chapter in this book about why we built it and what we were thinking when we did. Read it whenever you get there. It is not a sales pitch. It is the founder's honest account of what the credit repair industry looks like from the inside and why we decided to build something different.

Here is what this book covers and here is permission to read it in whatever order serves you best. The first section builds the technical foundation. How to use Claude to read your credit report and identify what is worth disputing. How the Section 609, 611, and 623 letters work and how to build each one with Claude in a single session. How to run a debt validation campaign against collectors who cannot prove what they claim you owe. How to negotiate directly with creditors when negotiation is the better path than dispute. If you are in the early stages of addressing damaged credit and you need the mechanics first, start at chapter one and move straight through.

If you are further along in your financial recovery and what you need is the current intelligence on how the rules changed and what those changes mean for your specific situation, jump to the back half. The chapters on FICO 10 and VantageScore 4.0 trended data will change how you think about mortgage preparation. The medical debt sweep chapter will tell you whether entries that should have come off your report already have. The chapter on new lending regulations and fintech risk will give you the analytical framework to evaluate any loan offer that comes your way as your score recovers and lenders start finding you. The business credit chapter will show you how to build a credit profile for your business that operates completely separately from your personal file. The chapter on cash management and life after credit repair addresses the question that almost no credit repair book asks, which is what you do with your financial life once the score is no longer the emergency.

There are also chapters in this book that are not in any other credit repair book on the market right now. The chapter on Special Purpose Credit Programs and recent ECOA amendments gives you access to lending pathways that standard credit score gatekeeping cannot reach. The chapter on the seven-year obsolescence audit gives you a mathematical tool for identifying illegal date manipulation in collection accounts. The chapter on student loan servicing errors covers a category of dispute that affects millions of borrowers and that most dispute guides ignore entirely because the complexity makes it easier to say there is nothing you can do, which is not accurate.

This book was written for people who are still recovering from pandemic-era financial disruption, from inflation that outran income for three consecutive years, from the economic conditions that created the highest consumer debt levels in American history. You are not alone in that recovery and the fact that your credit file reflects a difficult period does not mean the difficult period defines you permanently. Credit files change. Scores move. Entries age off. New positive history accumulates. The legal system gives you tools to accelerate that process and this book teaches you how to use them with the most capable AI reasoning tool available to a consumer today.

Read what resonates. Use what applies. Come back to the rest when your situation reaches the chapter that addresses it. This book is meant to be a resource you return to at different stages of the process, not a linear experience you complete once and set aside. The chapter that does not apply to you today may be exactly what you need six months from now when your score crosses a threshold that opens new decisions and new risks simultaneously.

We wrote this with Claude. We built Federal 609 with the same conviction that drives the writing, which is that information and tools that were previously available only to people who could afford professional help should be available to anyone willing to spend a few hours and less than a hundred dollars taking their financial life back into their own hands. That conviction is the whole project. This book is the latest expression of it. Go to federal609.com when you are ready to generate your letters. Everything else is in the chapters that follow.

1

Credit Repair 2026 with Claude: How We Built Federal 609, Wrote the Book, and Gave the Tools Back to the People

This chapter is different from every other chapter in this book. It is not about statute citations or dispute mechanics. It is about why any of this exists.

For years the credit repair industry operated on a simple and largely unspoken arrangement. The people who most needed help with their credit were also the people least likely to know their rights under federal law, and that knowledge gap was worth money to anyone willing to charge for access to it. Credit repair companies built businesses on the distance between what consumers did not know and what the law actually provided for free. They charged monthly fees ranging from fifty dollars to two hundred dollars or more to send letters that any consumer could send themselves, to dispute information that federal law already gave every American the right to dispute at no cost, and to provide access to a process that required nothing more than a stamp, a certified mail receipt, and knowledge of which statute to cite.

The founder of POPR Technologies lived on the receiving end of that arrangement for longer than he would like to count. Not because he was not smart enough to figure it out. Because the information was not presented in a way that made it accessible, and the industry that profits from that inaccessibility has very little incentive to change it. That experience is the origin of Federal 609 and understanding it honestly is the only way to understand what the platform is actually trying to do and why the approach we took is different from what exists in the market.

Federal 609 started as a book. Credit Repair 2026 with ChatGPT was written to give people the knowledge framework, the legal foundation, and the strategic understanding to approach their own credit repair with confidence. That book works and the organic sales it generated from the moment it landed on Amazon without a single dollar of advertising proved that the demand for honest, accessible credit repair information is real and significant and largely unmet by what currently exists. But a book has a limitation that became clear quickly. A reader can finish a book, understand everything in it, and still feel uncertain about the specific letter they need to send for their specific situation to their specific bureau for their specific account. The knowledge is there. The execution step feels like a gap.

Federal 609 closes that gap. It is a browser-based application that takes the legal framework from the book, the statute citations, the letter structures, the dispute strategies, and turns them into a four-step process that produces a personalized, legally grounded dispute letter in the time it takes to fill out a form. The user enters their information. They enter their dispute items. They review the strategy the application recommends based on what they entered. They download the letter. They print it, sign it, and mail it certified. The entire process costs nothing for the first letter and a fraction of what a monthly credit repair subscription costs for a complete dispute package covering multiple items across all three bureaus.

The decision to build it browser-based with no server storage was not primarily a technical decision. It was a values decision. The people using this application are entering sensitive personal information including the last four digits of their Social Security number, their date of birth, their address, and their account details. Storing that information on a server creates a database of financially vulnerable people's most sensitive data, which is exactly the kind of database that gets breached, sold, or misused. When the application runs entirely in the user's browser and the session clears when the tab closes, there is no database. There is nothing to breach. There is nothing to sell. The user's information exists only on their own device for the duration of their session and nowhere else. That is not a feature we added because it made the product more competitive. It is the only approach we were willing to build.

The pricing architecture was designed around the same principle. The free tier is real. A user who comes to Federal 609 and wants one Section 609 discovery request letter addressed to one bureau for one dispute item can get that letter for free, delivered to their email, without entering a credit card number. That is the promise and it is kept on every visit. The paid tiers exist because building and maintaining the platform requires resources and the goal was never to build a charity. It was to build the most affordable legitimate access point to the credit dispute process that the economics of running a real product allow. At $9.99 for up to three items across all three bureaus, the Starter plan costs less than an hour of a credit repair company's monthly fee. At $24.99 for up to ten items, the Standard plan costs less than most people spend on a single dinner out. At $99.99 for up to fifty items and a 30-day session restore that lets users come back across multiple sittings without losing their work, the Max Plan costs less than a single month with most credit repair companies and delivers more letters than most credit repair companies produce in six months of service.

The session restore system is worth explaining because it addresses something the credit repair industry almost never acknowledges which is that people's lives are complicated and financial administrative tasks compete with work, family, health, and everything else that demands attention in a given day. A user who starts the Federal 609 process at lunch, gets pulled into an afternoon of obligations, and comes back to finish that evening should not have to start over. The 30-day restore link that arrives by email after a paid session means that a user's work is preserved and available on any device through a secure link for a full month after payment. The session is theirs. The letters are theirs. The process accommodates real life rather than demanding that real life accommodate the process.

The connection between this platform and this book is not incidental. The book teaches you to understand what you are doing and why the law supports you in doing it. The platform does the letter generation so that understanding translates immediately into action. The design intention is that a reader finishes a chapter, understands the legal argument, goes to federal609.com, and generates the specific letter that chapter described within the same sitting. The book and the app are one system expressed in two forms and the combination is what makes the full credit repair process accessible to someone without legal training, without a credit repair company, and without more than a few hours of focused effort spread across whatever timeline their life allows.

POPR Technologies is a small company. It is not a venture-backed startup with a marketing budget and a growth team. It is a founder with a publishing background, a lived experience of financial hardship and recovery, and a conviction that the tools to navigate the credit system should not cost more than the system already costs the people who need them most. The books that InvestAI Publishing produces, the applications that POPR Technologies builds, and the AI systems that support both are all expressions of the same underlying position which is that information asymmetry is one of the most consequential forms of inequity in consumer finance and that reducing it is worth building a company around. Federal 609 is what that conviction looks like when it is expressed as a working product rather than a stated value.

If you read this book, used the Claude prompts, sent your dispute letters, and got results, you did it yourself. The law gave you the right. The knowledge gave you the capability. The platform gave you the tool. The credit repair industry would have charged you a monthly subscription for access to the same process. We wanted to see what happened if we charged you as little as possible and gave you as much as possible and trusted you to handle the rest. The answer, based on the organic response to the first book and the early users of the platform, is that people handle it exactly as well as they would have if they had paid ten times more for the same access. That result is not surprising to us. It probably should not be surprising to anyone.

federal609.com
Fix Your Credit. Know the Law.

2

How to Use Claude AI to Fix Your Credit: Why It Works Differently Than Any Tool You Have Used Before

Most people who try to use AI to fix their credit get the same result. A generic letter. A paragraph that sounds official but has no real information in it. A response that could apply to anyone.

That is not a problem with AI. That is a problem with how they used it.

Claude is not a search engine. When you type a question into Google, it finds pages that contain answers. Claude does something different. Claude reads what you give it, holds that information in memory, and reasons through it to build a specific response. The output is only as specific as what you put in. That is the rule. It does not change.

This matters for credit repair because your dispute letter is not generic. Your dispute letter has your name, your address, a specific creditor, a specific account number, a specific reason for disputing, and a specific legal argument. A generic letter has none of that. Bureaus know the difference. They look for any reason to call a dispute frivolous. A letter that could have been written for anyone is easy to ignore.

Claude will not ignore your specifics. Claude cannot. Every detail you give it becomes part of the reasoning. The more precise you are, the more precise the output. That is the tool you are working with.

Why Claude Holds Context and What That Means for Your Letters

Context is the single most important word in this book.

When you open a Claude session and start typing, Claude reads everything in that conversation. Your name. Your address. The creditor. The account number. The balance. The date the account went delinquent. The bureau reporting it. The reason you believe the entry is wrong. All of it stays active as long as the conversation is open.

That means when you ask Claude to write your dispute letter, Claude is not guessing at the details. Claude already has them. The letter comes out with your information in every field because Claude read every field you gave it.

Compare that to a template you download from the internet. The template has brackets where your information goes. You fill them in. Sometimes you miss one. Sometimes the bracket language does not match your situation. The letter goes out looking like what it is: a form that someone filled in.

A bureau cannot tell the difference between a form letter and a Claude letter from the outside. But inside, the difference is significant. Claude letters cite the specific statute for your specific dispute type. Claude letters name the specific creditor and account. Claude letters use the specific language that triggers a legal obligation on the bureau's part. That specificity is what makes the letter harder to dismiss.

The Three Things to Paste In Before You Ask Claude Anything

Before you ask Claude to write a single word of your dispute letter, give it three things. In order. Do not skip any of them.

First: the account entry exactly as it appears on your credit report. Copy and paste the text directly from the bureau's report. Every field. Account name, account number, account type, payment status, date opened, date of last activity, date of first delinquency if shown, reported balance, credit limit if applicable, and which bureau you pulled this from. If the report shows a payment history grid, describe what you see. Thirty days late in March 2024. Sixty days late in April 2024. Whatever it shows.

Second: your dispute reason in plain language. Do not use legal terms yet. Just say what you believe is wrong. The balance is wrong. This account is not mine. This debt was paid in full in 2023. I filed bankruptcy and this was included in the discharge. I am a victim of identity theft. Plain language. Claude translates it into legal language in the letter. You just have to tell Claude what you know.

Third: your goal. What do you want to happen? You want the item deleted. You want the balance corrected. You want the payment history updated. You want a late payment removed. State it clearly. Claude writes toward that goal.

That is the setup. Once Claude has those three things, you ask for the letter and Claude builds it.

CLAUDE PROMPT — CHAPTER 1 SETUP

I am working on a credit dispute and I need your help writing a dispute letter. I am going to give you three things before I ask you to write anything. First: here is the account entry from my credit report exactly as it appears. [Paste the full account entry here.] Second: here is my dispute reason in plain language. [Describe what you believe is wrong.] Third: here is my goal. [State what you want the bureau to do.] Do not write the letter yet. Read everything I gave you and confirm you have what you need. Ask me if anything is missing.

Why Shorter Prompts Produce Worse Letters

The most common mistake people make with Claude and credit repair is the short prompt.

They type: write me a 609 letter.

Claude writes a 609 letter. It has the statute citation. It has the formal language. It has the correct structure. And it has blank lines where the creditor name, account number, and personal information should go because Claude has no idea what those are.

That letter is useless. Not because Claude did anything wrong. Because the input was empty.

There is a direct relationship between the length of what you give Claude and the quality of what Claude gives back. This is not a flaw in the system. This is the system working correctly. Claude builds from what you provide. If you provide nothing, Claude builds from nothing.

The prompts in this book are long on purpose. They are structured on purpose. They ask you to paste in actual text from your credit report on purpose. Every piece of information you give Claude is a piece of your dispute letter that does not require guessing.

Do not shorten the prompts. Do not summarize. Paste the actual text. Give Claude the real numbers. That is the difference between a letter that looks like it was generated by a machine and a letter that looks like it was written by someone who knows exactly what they are disputing and why.

How to Tell When Claude Is Reasoning Versus When It Is Guessing

Claude will always produce a response. That is worth knowing before you rely on anything it writes.

When Claude has enough information, it reasons. The response is specific. The creditor name is in the letter. The account number is in the letter. The statute cited matches your dispute type. The tone and language match the legal obligation you are invoking.

When Claude does not have enough information, it fills in gaps. It uses placeholder language. It writes the letter with a generic creditor name. It uses the most common statute rather than the most appropriate one. It sounds correct but applies to everyone and therefore applies to no one.

You can tell the difference by reading the output critically. If the letter looks like it could be sent to any bureau for any account by any person, Claude did not have enough to work with. Go back. Add more detail. Paste the actual account entry. Describe the dispute reason more specifically. Ask Claude what else it needs.

Claude will tell you what is missing if you ask. After you give it the setup, ask: what information do you still need to write the most accurate dispute letter possible? Claude will answer that question. Whatever it asks for, give it.

The One Thing Claude Will Not Do and Why That Protects You

Claude will not contact the credit bureaus for you.

Claude will not submit your dispute online. Claude will not make phone calls. Claude will not sign your letter. Claude will not mail anything.

This is not a limitation. This is the law working in your favor.

Under the Fair Credit Reporting Act, a dispute has legal weight when it comes from the consumer directly. When you sign the letter and mail it certified with return receipt requested, you create a legal record. The bureau received your dispute on a specific date. They are now on the 30 day clock. If they fail to respond, that failure is a violation of federal law and you have the documentation to prove it.

A dispute submitted through a third party, including a credit repair company, does not carry the same weight. The FCRA treats direct consumer disputes as the highest priority. Credit repair company disputes can be deprioritized. Some bureaus have policies that allow them to flag disputes from companies rather than consumers.

Claude writes the letter. You print it, sign it, and mail it. That sequence matters. It puts the legal record in your hands and your hands only.

CLAUDE PROMPT — FULL CHAPTER 1 LETTER BUILD

I have given you my account entry, my dispute reason, and my goal. Now write me a formal dispute letter. Address it to: [Bureau name and address]. Send it as: a Section 611 reinvestigation demand citing 15 U.S.C. Section 1681i. Include: my name [name], my address [address], the account name [name], the account number [number], and my specific dispute reason. Close with: a statement that I expect written results within 30 days per federal law. Format: formal business letter. No brackets or placeholders. Write every field from what I gave you.

You have the Claude prompt. Now get the letter. Go to federal609.com and generate your free Section 609 discovery request in 4 steps. The app builds the letter from your inputs. You download it, print it, sign it, and mail it certified. That is the whole process.

Claude is the reasoning engine. Federal 609 is the generation engine. Your signature is the legal instrument.

The bureaus have 30 days once your letter arrives. That clock does not start until you mail it.

3

What Your Credit Report Is Actually Saying and How Claude Reads It When You Cannot

The numbers are not random. Here is the translation.

You have seen your credit report. Most people look at it the same way they look at a utility bill in a foreign language. They know it matters. They cannot read it.

The bureaus designed it that way. Not accidentally. The harder the file is to read, the less likely you are to dispute what is wrong in it. Confusion is the first line of defense.

Claude reads it differently. When you paste an account entry into Claude, Claude does not see a wall of codes and dates. Claude sees a sequence of data points with legal implications. It reads the account status and knows which statute applies. It reads the date of first delinquency and calculates whether the item is past the seven year reporting limit. It reads the payment history grid and flags inconsistencies that human eyes miss on the first pass.

This chapter teaches you what to give Claude so that it can do that work for you.

What the Account Status Codes Actually Mean

Every account on your credit report has a status. The status tells the bureau, the lender, and Claude what the current condition of that account is. Most people never look at it. It is one of the most important fields on the page.

Current means the account is open and payments are being made on time. This is neutral or positive depending on what else is in the file.

Closed means the account is no longer active. Closed does not mean removed. A closed account stays on your report for up to ten years if it was positive and seven years if it was negative.

Charged off means the original creditor gave up on collecting and wrote the debt off as a loss. The debt does not disappear. The creditor typically sells it to a collection agency. The charge off notation stays on your report for seven years from the date of first delinquency, not from the date the creditor charged it off. That distinction matters for disputes.

In collections means a third party now owns or is servicing the debt. This generates a separate entry on your report from the collection account, which often appears in addition to the original creditor's entry. Two entries for one debt. Both reportable. Both disputable if either contains an error.

The Date of First Delinquency: The Most Important Date on Your Report

The date of first delinquency is the date you first missed a payment and never caught up. It is not the date the account was charged off. It is not the date the collector bought the debt. It is not the date of last activity. It is the date the account first went past due on the path that led to the negative status.

That date controls everything. The seven year reporting clock starts there.

Creditors and collectors sometimes report the wrong date. They report a later date so the item stays on your report longer. This is one of the most common errors in credit reporting and one of the most disputable.

Claude calculates this for you. Give Claude the date of first delinquency as reported and Claude tells you whether the item should still be on your report. If it should not, Claude writes the dispute letter citing the obsolescence rule under 15 U.S.C. Section 1681c.

What Re-Aging Is and How to Spot It Before You Know the Term

Re-aging is when a creditor or collector reports a more recent date of first delinquency than the real one. The effect is that the seven year clock resets. An item that should have fallen off your report in 2022 now shows a 2024 delinquency date and stays until 2031.

Re-aging is illegal under the FCRA. It is also common.

You do not need to know the legal term to spot it. You just need to notice when the date feels wrong. If a debt is old but the delinquency date on the report looks recent, that is the signal. Paste the entry into Claude and ask.

Claude will tell you whether the date is consistent with the account history, whether the timeline makes legal sense, and whether the entry has grounds for a dispute based on the reported dates alone.

How to Read the Payment History Grid

The payment history grid is the row of symbols or codes that shows your payment status month by month going back up to seven years. Different bureaus display it differently. Some use symbols. Some use numbers. Some use color coding that does not survive a PDF printout.

OK or a checkmark means on time. 30 means thirty days late. 60 means sixty days late. 90 means ninety days late. 120 and beyond means seriously delinquent.

What Claude looks for in the grid is internal consistency. If an account shows a charge off status in June 2022 but the grid shows on time payments through August 2022, something is wrong. The timeline is contradictory. That contradiction is disputable. A bureau cannot verify an entry that contradicts itself.

Describe the grid to Claude in plain language. Tell Claude what month showed what status. Claude will identify the inconsistency and name the statute that applies.

How Claude Compares All Three Bureau Reports Simultaneously

The same account often reports differently across Equifax, Experian, and TransUnion. Different balances. Different dates. Different account statuses. Different payment histories.

Each inconsistency is a separate dispute opportunity.

If Equifax shows a balance of four thousand dollars and TransUnion shows a balance of six thousand dollars on the same account, one of them is wrong. If Experian shows the account as open and Equifax shows it as closed, one of them is wrong. Inaccuracy does not require fraud. It just requires one bureau reporting something different from what the creditor actually reports to all three.

Start a Claude session with all three entries side by side. Ask Claude to compare them and identify every inconsistency. Then ask Claude to prioritize which inconsistency has the strongest legal grounds for a dispute. Start there.

CLAUDE PROMPT CHAPTER 2

I am going to paste three entries for the same account from three different credit bureaus.
Read all three carefully. Then tell me:

1. What the date of first delinquency is on each report and whether they are consistent.
2. Whether this item should still be on my report based on the 7 year FCRA rule under 15 U.S.C. Section 1681c.
3. Every inconsistency you find across the three entries — balance, status, dates, payment history.
4. Which inconsistency has the strongest grounds for a dispute letter.

Before you run this prompt, pull your credit reports from AnnualCreditReport.com. That is the only federally authorized free source. Pull all three bureaus at once. Once you have the reports open, find the account you want to dispute and copy the full entry from each bureau exactly as it appears. Then paste each one where the prompt asks for it.

Do not write a letter yet. Just give me the analysis.

FEDERAL 609

The Federal 609 app reads your dispute item entries and recommends the correct letter type based on what you input. Go to federal609.com.

Enter the account in Step 2. The app does the analysis automatically. Get your free Section 609 letter and see exactly what the bureau is required to show you about that account.

The credit report is not a verdict. It is a dataset. Datasets have errors. Federal law gives you the right to correct them.

Claude finds the errors. The letters force the correction. The clock starts when the certified mail lands.

4

The Section 609 Letter: What It Is, What It Forces the Bureau to Do, and How to Get Yours Free

Most people selling 609 letters online charge fifty dollars for something you are about to understand in ten minutes.

There is more myth around the Section 609 letter than almost any other topic in credit repair.

People sell them as a secret loophole. They are not. People claim they erase any debt automatically. They do not. People say bureaus are legally required to delete anything they cannot prove you signed for. That is a misreading of the statute that has been circulating online for years and has cost a lot of people a lot of money and time chasing something that does not work the way it was described to them.

Here is what Section 609 actually does. It forces the bureau to show you everything in your consumer file. Where the information came from. Who it was shared with. What they have on you. That is the disclosure. That disclosure is what you use to build your real dispute under Section 611. The

609 letter opens the file. The 611 letter closes the fight. You need both and you need them in the right order.

This chapter builds the 609 letter with Claude and shows you exactly where to get it generated for free.

What 15 U.S.C. Section 1681g Actually Says

Section 1681g is the statute behind every 609 letter. In plain language it requires any consumer reporting agency to disclose to you, upon request, the complete contents of your consumer file. Every piece of information they hold about you. Every source they got it from. Every person or entity that received a consumer report containing your information in the past two years for employment purposes, and the past five years for any other purpose.

That is significant. The bureau must tell you not just what is in your file but where it came from and who has seen it.

That disclosure is intelligence. When you know the source of a negative entry, you know who to send your Section 623 furnisher dispute to. When you know who has accessed your file, you can identify unauthorized inquiries. When you have the complete file in writing, you have a baseline to compare against any future changes.

The bureau has fifteen business days to respond to a Section 609 request. Not calendar days. Business days. Keep that distinction when you are counting down the clock.

Why This Letter Comes First

The dispute sequence matters. Most people skip the 609 and go straight to a

611 reinvestigation demand. That is not wrong. A 611 dispute is legally valid without a prior 609 request. But sending the 609 first gives you something the 611 alone does not: a documented record of what the bureau claims is in your file before you dispute it.

If the bureau later says an item was verified, you have the disclosure showing exactly what information they held at the time of your request. If the disclosure they sent you is incomplete or contradicts what they later claim they verified against, that inconsistency is your evidence.

The 609 is a reconnaissance letter. It tells you what you are dealing with before you commit to a full dispute campaign. Send it first. Read what comes back. Then build your 611 with the actual information the bureau gave you.

What the Bureau Sends Back and What to Do With It

When the bureau responds to your 609 request, you will receive a document that is either a full file disclosure or something that falls short of it. Both are useful.

A full file disclosure shows every account in your file, the source of each entry, the inquiry history, and the recipients of your report. Read it line by line against the credit report you pulled from AnnualCreditReport.com. Look for accounts that appear in the disclosure but not on your report. Look for sources listed for entries you believe are inaccurate. Look for inquiries from companies you never gave permission to access your file.

If the bureau sends back something incomplete, that is a different opportunity. A bureau that fails to provide the full disclosure you requested under Section 1681g has violated a federal obligation. Document the date you sent the request and the date you received the response. Document what was missing. That documentation becomes the basis for a CFPB complaint and, if necessary, a litigation notice.

Either outcome moves you forward. That is why you send it.

CLAUDE PROMPT

Help me write a Section 609 disclosure request letter to [Equifax / Experian / TransUnion].

Here is my information:

- Full name: [your name]
- Current mailing address: [your address]
- Date of birth: [your date of birth]
- Last four digits of Social Security Number: [last four only]

I am requesting the following under 15 U.S.C. Section 1681g:

1. The complete contents of my consumer file.
2. The identity of every source from which information in my file was obtained.
3. The identity of every person or entity that received a consumer report

containing my information in the past two years for employment purposes and the past five years for any other purpose.

4. All soft inquiries on my file.

Format this as a formal business letter. Address it to the correct bureau address. Close with a statement that I expect their response within 15 business days per federal law. Do not include any placeholder brackets in the final letter.

"'

Send this prompt three times, once for each bureau. Change the bureau name and address each time. Mail each letter certified with return receipt requested on the same day. Keep the tracking numbers. The 15 day clock starts on the date of delivery, not the date you mailed it.

—-

The bureau addresses for certified mail are as follows. Equifax Information Services LLC, P.O. Box 740241, Atlanta, GA 30374. Experian, P.O. Box 4500, Allen, TX 75013. TransUnion LLC Consumer Dispute Center, P.O. Box 2000, Chester, PA 19016.

Write those down. Save them somewhere you will not lose them. Every letter in this book goes to one or more of those three addresses.

—-

FEDERAL 609 | The Federal 609 app generates your Section 609 disclosure request in four steps. Go to federal609.com. Enter your information. The app builds the letter. You download it, print it, sign it, and mail it certified. Your first letter is free. No account required. No credit card required to start. The app does in four steps what this chapter just taught you in ten minutes.

—-

The 609 letter does one job. It opens the file.

What the bureau sends back tells you what you are actually fighting. Read it carefully. Bring it to Chapter 4.

5

How to Write a Section 611 Dispute Letter That Forces the Bureau to Investigate or Delete

The Section 609 letter asked the bureau to show you the file. The Section 611 letter tells the bureau something in that file is wrong and demands they prove otherwise.

That is a different kind of letter. It is not a request. It is a legal demand with a federal deadline attached to it.

Under 15 U.S.C. Section 1681i, when a consumer disputes the accuracy or completeness of any item in their credit file, the bureau must conduct a reasonable reinvestigation within 30 days. If they cannot verify the item through that reinvestigation, they must delete it or correct it. Not at their discretion. Not when they get around to it. They must.

That word must is why the 611 letter is the most powerful tool in this book.

What Reasonable Reinvestigation Actually Means

The FCRA requires a reasonable reinvestigation. The bureau interprets that word as loosely as the law allows.

Here is what typically happens. The bureau sends an automated data verification request to the furnisher, the company that reported the negative item. The furnisher's system responds with a code confirming the information. The bureau marks the item verified. The whole process takes a few minutes. Nobody looked at a document. Nobody pulled an account record. Nobody checked whether the date of first delinquency is accurate or whether the balance matches the original agreement.

That process satisfies the bureau's internal standard. Whether it satisfies the legal standard of reasonable is a different question, and it is a question courts have answered in favor of consumers in cases where the dispute was specific and documented.

The more specific your 611 letter is, the harder it is for an automated response to satisfy the reinvestigation requirement. A letter that says this account is wrong gives the furnisher's system something easy to confirm. A letter that says this account reports a date of first delinquency of March 2021 but I have a payment confirmation showing a payment was made in February 2021 which means the delinquency date is wrong and the seven year clock is running from the incorrect date requires an actual human to look at an actual record to respond.

Write specific 611 letters. Claude helps you do that.

What to Include in Every Section 611 Letter

Your full legal name and current mailing address go at the top of every letter. The bureau needs to match your letter to your file. If your name or address does not match what they have on record, they can delay processing by claiming they cannot identify the consumer. Do not give them that opening.

Include the last four digits of your Social Security number and your date of birth. Again, matching. Not because you are required to give this information in full, but because matching accelerates the process and removes any procedural excuse for delay.

Name the specific account you are disputing. Creditor name. Account number, or the last four digits if you do not have the full number. The balance as reported. Which bureau you are writing to. Do not send a blanket dispute covering multiple accounts in a single letter. Send one letter per account, or at minimum make the accounts clearly separated within the letter. A multi-item dispute letter that is vague gives the bureau room to address one item and ignore the others.

State your dispute reason precisely. Not this account is wrong. This account reports a balance of four thousand two hundred dollars. The correct balance as of my last statement, which I can provide, is two thousand eight hundred dollars. The difference of one thousand four hundred dollars is unsubstantiated and I am requesting written documentation of how this balance was calculated.

Cite the statute. Every 611 letter cites 15 U.S.C. Section 1681i. Every letter states that you expect written results of the reinvestigation within 30 days of the bureau's receipt of this letter. Every letter is sent certified with return receipt requested.

Attach documentation when you have it. A paid receipt. A bank statement showing payment. A court order. A bankruptcy discharge document. A letter from the original creditor. Whatever supports your position. Documentation does not guarantee deletion but it makes the automated verification response significantly harder to sustain.

The 45 Day Extension and When It Applies

The standard reinvestigation window is 30 days. There is one exception. If you provide additional relevant information within the investigation period, the bureau gets an additional 15 days to complete the investigation. That extension is not a penalty to you. It is an acknowledgment that new documentation requires more time to evaluate.

Use this strategically. If you have documentation that supports your dispute, send it with the initial letter. You want the bureau to have everything they need to verify your position. If the documentation is strong enough, the investigation may resolve in your favor before the 45 days are up. If it does not, you now have a clear record of what you submitted and when, which becomes your evidence if you escalate.

What Cannot Be Verified Means and Why It Results in Mandatory Deletion

If the bureau completes its reinvestigation and cannot verify the accuracy of the disputed information, the FCRA is unambiguous. They must promptly delete the information or modify it if modification is what the facts support.

Cannot be verified does not require the information to be provably false. It requires only that the bureau cannot confirm it is accurate through a reasonable investigation. That is a lower bar than most people realize.

Old debts are often unverifiable. The original creditor sold the account years ago. The collector who bought it has records that are incomplete or inconsistent. The furnisher cannot produce the original signed agreement. The date of first delinquency on file does not match anything in the available records. Any of these conditions can result in a cannot be verified outcome.

When that happens, deletion is mandatory. Not optional. Not subject to negotiation. The item comes off.

CLAUDE PROMPT CHAPTER 4

I am disputing an account on my credit report under Section 611 of the FCRA, 15 U.S.C. Section 1681i. Here is everything you need to write the letter.

My information:

- Full name: [your name]
- Address: [your address]
- Date of birth: [your date of birth]
- Last four of SSN: [last four]

Account being disputed:

Creditor name: [creditor name]

Account number: [account number or last four]

Reported balance: [balance as shown on report]

Bureau I am writing to: [Equifax / Experian / TransUnion]

Date of first delinquency as reported: [date]

My dispute reason, in detail:

[Describe exactly what is wrong. Be specific. Include dates, amounts, and any documentation you have.]

My goal:

[Deletion / Balance correction / Status correction / Payment history correction]

Write a formal Section 611 reinvestigation demand letter.

Cite 15 U.S.C. Section 1681i specifically.

State that I expect written results within 30 days of receipt.

Include a sentence stating that if the item cannot be verified through reasonable reinvestigation, it must be deleted per federal law.

No brackets. No placeholders. Write every field from what I gave you.

When the Bureau Writes Back

Two things can happen. The bureau conducts the investigation and resolves the dispute in your favor. The item is deleted or corrected and you receive written confirmation. Pull your updated report 30 days after that confirmation to verify the change actually appears.

Or the bureau writes back and says the item was verified. That response is not the end. It is the beginning of the next phase. Chapter 18 covers exactly what to do when a bureau claims verified and why that response often creates more legal exposure for them than it closes for you.

What you do not do is accept the result and stop. Verified means someone at the furnisher responded to an automated data request. It does not mean the information is accurate. It does not mean the investigation was reasonable. It means the process ran its course and produced an output. Your job is to determine whether that output holds up under scrutiny.

FEDERAL 609 | The Federal 609 app generates your Section 611 reinvestigation demand at federal609.com. After your free Section 609 letter, upgrade to get the full dispute stack for your accounts across all three bureaus. The app reads your dispute reason and recommends the right letter type. You download, print, sign, and mail.

Thirty days is the bureau's window. Not yours. Yours starts the day they receive the letter and does not close until the item is gone or the dispute is escalated.

Keep the tracking number. Keep the certified mail receipt. Keep a copy of everything you sent. The paper trail is the case.

6

How to Dispute Directly with the Creditor Using Section 623 and Why This Letter Changes the Pressure

The bureau is not the only one with a legal obligation. The company that reported the error has one too.

Most people send their dispute to the bureau and wait. That is half the strategy.

The other half goes directly to the company that put the negative item on your report in the first place. That company is called a furnisher. Every bank, credit card company, medical provider, auto lender, and collection agency that reports information to the bureaus is a furnisher. And furnishers have their own investigation obligation under federal law that is completely separate from what the bureaus are required to do.

Section 623 of the FCRA, codified at 15 U.S.C. Section 1681s-2, requires furnishers who receive notice of a dispute to conduct their own investigation, review all relevant information, and correct or delete any inaccurate information they find. That obligation is not triggered by your dispute with the bureau. It is triggered by a direct dispute letter sent to the furnisher itself.

This means you can apply legal pressure from two directions simultaneously. The bureau investigates from one side. The furnisher investigates from the other. Most negative items cannot survive that.

Why Direct Furnisher Disputes Work Differently

When you dispute through the bureau, the bureau contacts the furnisher electronically. The furnisher's system responds with a code. The bureau marks the item verified. The whole process is automated and takes minutes.

When you dispute directly with the furnisher, a human being at that company is supposed to receive your letter, pull the account file, review the documentation you provided, and make a determination about whether the information they are reporting is accurate. The legal standard is different. The process is different. The outcome can be different.

Furnishers also have something the bureaus do not: the original account records. The signed agreement. The payment history in their own system. The notes on the account. If the error originated with the furnisher, the furnisher is the only party who can actually fix it at the source. A bureau can delete an entry, but if the furnisher keeps reporting the same inaccurate information, it can reappear. Going directly to the furnisher fixes the problem where it starts.

Finding the Right Address

The furnisher dispute address is not the billing address. It is not the customer service address. It is a specific address designated for written disputes under the FCRA.

Most large creditors publish this address on their website under a section titled something like legal notices or disputes or consumer rights. If you cannot find it, call the creditor's main number and ask specifically for the address where you should send a written FCRA dispute. Write down the name of the person you spoke with and the date. That documentation matters if there is ever a question about whether you sent the dispute to the right place.

Claude can help you locate furnisher dispute addresses if you give it the creditor name. Ask Claude directly: what is the FCRA dispute address for [creditor name]. Claude may have this information or may tell you to verify it directly with the creditor. Either way, do not send the letter to the wrong address. A dispute sent to the billing department is not a legal dispute under Section 623. It is a complaint letter that carries no federal weight.

When to Send 611 and 623 at the Same Time

Send both letters on the same day whenever you can. There is no legal reason to wait for the bureau's response before sending the furnisher dispute. The obligations are parallel, not sequential.

Sending both simultaneously does two things. It creates two separate investigation timelines running at the same time. And it signals to both parties that you understand your rights under both applicable sections of the FCRA. That signal matters. A consumer who clearly knows the law gets handled differently than a consumer who sends a vague complaint.

The 30 day investigation window applies to the furnisher as well. Under Regulation V, the CFPB's implementing regulation for Section 623, furnishers have 30 days to complete their investigation of a direct dispute. If they fail to respond or fail to correct an error they identify, that failure is separately actionable from any failure by the bureau.

Two timelines. Two legal obligations. One letter in each direction.

What Regulation V Requires

Regulation V is the CFPB rule that governs how furnishers handle disputes. It requires furnishers to establish and follow reasonable written policies and procedures for investigating direct disputes. It requires them to review all relevant information provided by the consumer. It requires them to correct, delete, or permanently block reporting of information they determine to be inaccurate.

The word permanently matters. If a furnisher determines through investigation that information they reported is inaccurate, they cannot simply correct it once and then re-report the same error. The correction has to hold. If the same inaccurate information reappears on your credit report after a furnisher investigation found it to be wrong, that reappearance is a Regulation V violation on top of an FCRA violation.

Document everything. Date every letter. Keep every response. Build the file as if every piece of paper will eventually be read by an attorney, because if this goes far enough, it will be.

CLAUDE PROMPT: CHAPTER 5

I want to send a Section 623 direct furnisher dispute letter to the company that is reporting a negative item on my credit report.

Here is my information:

- Full name: [your name]
- Address: [your address]

Here is the furnisher I am writing to:

Company name: [creditor or collector name]

Dispute address: [furnisher's FCRA dispute address]

Account number: [account number]

Here is what they are reporting:

Reported balance: [amount]

Account status: [charge off / collection / late payment / other]

Date of first delinquency as reported: [date]

Which bureaus are showing this: [list bureaus]

Here is my dispute reason in detail:

[Describe exactly what is wrong. Be specific. Include any documentation you have or plan to attach.]

Write a formal Section 623 direct dispute letter citing 15 U.S.C. Section

1681s-2(b) and Regulation V. State that I expect their written response

within 30 days. Include a paragraph stating that if they determine the information is inaccurate, they are required to correct or delete it permanently across all bureaus they report to. No placeholders.

Write every field from what I gave you.

What to Attach to the Letter

Include copies, never originals, of any documentation that supports your dispute. A bank statement showing a payment the furnisher claims was not made. A paid in full letter from the original creditor. A bankruptcy discharge document listing the account. A written agreement showing a different balance than what is being reported. A police report or FTC identity theft report if the account is fraudulent.

Every document you include narrows the furnisher's ability to call the dispute frivolous or unsubstantiated. A dispute with no documentation is a dispute based on your word. A dispute with a bank statement showing the payment is a dispute based on a paper record. Furnishers treat those two things very differently.

Send the letter and all attachments via certified mail with return receipt requested. Keep the tracking number. Keep a copy of everything you sent including the envelope it went out in if you can manage it.

FEDERAL 609 | The Federal 609 app generates Section 623 furnisher dispute letters as part of its paid letter packages. After you get your free Section 609 letter at federal609.com, upgrade to the Starter plan or above to access the full dispute stack including the direct furnisher letter. The app generates all letters from the same session so your information stays consistent across every letter in the package.

The bureau is one pressure point. The furnisher is another. Using both at the same time is not aggressive. It is the system working the way Congress designed it to work.

Send both letters. Keep both tracking numbers. The furnisher has 30 days the same as the bureau. Run the clocks together.

7

How to Use Claude to Identify Every Negative Item Worth Disputing: A Complete Strategy for Reading Your Credit File Like a Consumer Law Attorney

Not everything on your report is worth fighting. Here is how Claude tells the difference.

Before you write a single letter, you need a list. Not a vague sense that something looks wrong. A specific, prioritized list of every item on your credit report that has grounds for a dispute, ranked by how strong those grounds are and how much score impact the removal would produce. Claude builds that list for you in one session if you give it the right input.

Most people approach their credit report emotionally. They see a collection account from a hospital visit three years ago and they want it gone because it feels unfair. That reaction is understandable. It is also a poor dispute strategy. The strength of a dispute is not determined by how much the item bothers you. It is determined by whether the information as reported is accurate, complete, and within the legal reporting window. Emotion does not move bureaus. Statute citations do.

Claude removes the emotion from the process. When you paste an account entry into Claude and ask for a legal analysis, Claude does not care how the debt made you feel. Claude reads the dates, the balances, the account status, and the payment history and tells you whether any of those fields give you legal grounds to demand a correction or deletion. That objectivity is one of the most valuable things Claude brings to credit repair.

Start by pulling all three credit reports from AnnualCreditReport.com. Lay them side by side, either on screen or printed out. Go through every negative entry, meaning every account that is not showing as current and in good standing, and make a simple list. Creditor name, account number, which bureaus are reporting it, the reported balance, the account status, and the date of first delinquency if it is shown. That list is what you bring to Claude.

Once you have the list, open a Claude session and paste the first entry. Ask Claude four questions for every single item. First, is the date of first delinquency within the seven year reporting window under 15 U.S.C. Section 1681c. Second, is there any inconsistency between how this item is reported across the three bureaus. Third, does the account status as reported match what the payment history shows. Fourth, based on what is here, which dispute letter type gives me the strongest legal argument for removal or correction. Claude answers all four and tells you whether the item is worth disputing and why.

Go through every negative entry on the list this way before you write your first letter. By the time you finish, you will have a prioritized dispute strategy, not a stack of random letters. You will know which accounts have strong grounds, which have weak grounds, and which are accurately reported and not worth your time. That distinction matters because sending frivolous disputes damages your credibility with the bureaus and can make subsequent legitimate disputes harder to process.

The items worth disputing fall into categories. Obsolete items are accounts past the seven year reporting window that are still appearing. Inaccurate items are accounts where the balance, status, date, or payment history does not match the facts. Unverifiable items are accounts, often old collection accounts, where the furnisher likely no longer has the original records necessary to confirm the debt. Duplicate items are accounts appearing more than once on the same bureau report, which happens frequently when a debt is sold from one collector to another and both report it. Each category has a different dispute argument and Claude matches the argument to the category automatically when you give it enough detail.

After Claude analyzes each item, ask it one more question before moving to the letter stage. Ask Claude which of these accounts is causing the most damage to my credit score right now and which removal would produce the fastest score improvement. Claude cannot access your live score but it can reason about impact based on what you describe. A recent collection account with a high balance hitting all three bureaus is more damaging than a single late payment from six years ago on one bureau. Removing the most damaging item first produces the fastest visible improvement. That sequence keeps you motivated through a process that can take months.

One category deserves special attention and that is the category Claude flags as potentially unverifiable. These are the disputes with the highest probability of resulting in deletion without a prolonged fight. Old collection accounts, especially those that have changed hands multiple times, are frequently impossible to verify because the documentation chain breaks down every time the debt is sold. The collector reporting the item today may have bought it from a collector who bought it from the original creditor years ago. What they have is a spreadsheet entry with your name and a balance. What they do not have is the original signed agreement, a complete payment history, or documentation that ties the reported balance to the original debt amount. When the bureau sends the verification request and the collector cannot produce that documentation, the item cannot be verified. Mandatory deletion follows.

Claude identifies these accounts by looking at the age of the debt, the number of times it has changed hands if that information is visible in the report, and the reported balance relative to what an original debt in that category typically looks like. It is not a perfect system but it is a significantly better starting point than guessing. Go to federal609.com after this session and generate your free Section 609 disclosure request. The disclosure the bureau sends back will show you exactly who reported each entry and when, which gives you even more information to bring back to Claude for the next round of analysis.

The goal of this chapter is to walk into Chapter 7 with a completed dispute list, not a stack of feelings about your credit report. Claude is the tool that gets you there. The letters are what you do with the list once it exists.

8

What the Trump-Era Credit Rule Changes Actually Mean for Your Dispute in 2026 and 2027: How Federal Policy Shifts Change the Letters You Send and the Results You Can Expect

The rules changed. Most people disputing right now do not know which ones.

The credit reporting landscape that exists in 2026 is not the same one that existed three years ago. Court decisions vacated rules the CFPB spent years building. Administrative priorities shifted. Enforcement postures changed. Some of those changes helped consumers. Some of them removed protections that people were counting on. If you are sending dispute letters based on information you read online in 2022 or 2023, some of what you think you know is no longer accurate and some of the leverage you think you have may have been reduced or eliminated by decisions made in federal courtrooms and agency offices since then.

This chapter does not take a political position on any of those changes. The changes happened. They affect your dispute strategy. You need to know what they are.

The most significant shift for consumers disputing medical debt is the court decision that vacated the CFPB rule that would have removed most medical debt from credit reports. That rule, which was finalized in early 2025, would have eliminated medical debt under five hundred dollars from reports entirely and removed medical debt as a factor in credit scoring models. A federal court struck it down before it fully took effect. The practical result is that medical debt is still reportable in most circumstances, the previous rules still govern how and when it can appear, and consumers who were waiting for automatic removal need to shift strategy and dispute these accounts the way they would dispute any other negative entry, which means statute citations, specific dispute reasons, and certified mail.

The student loan picture is similarly complicated. Federal student loan payment pauses ended. Missed payments during the transition period between pause and resumption created new derogatory entries for borrowers who did not realize their payments had restarted or whose servicers did not communicate the restart clearly. Those transition period entries are worth examining closely because servicer communication failures during a policy transition are exactly the kind of factual dispute that holds up under a Section 611 reinvestigation. If you missed payments because your servicer failed to notify you that the pause had ended, that is not a payment history dispute. That is a furnisher accuracy dispute and Claude helps you frame it that way.

CFPB enforcement posture matters because it affects how aggressively the bureaus comply with consumer disputes. During periods of active CFPB enforcement, bureaus tend to resolve disputes more carefully because the cost of a CFPB complaint landing with real investigative follow-up is significant. During periods of reduced enforcement, bureaus have less external pressure to move quickly or thoroughly on individual disputes. That does not change your legal rights. Your rights under the FCRA are statutory, meaning they come from the law itself and do not disappear when an administration changes enforcement priorities. What it does change is your escalation strategy. In a lower enforcement environment, CFPB complaints carry less immediate pressure than they did in prior years, which means your dispute letters need to be more specific, more documented, and more clearly structured around the legal argument from the beginning rather than relying on regulatory pressure to close the gap.

The practical adjustment is this. Write tighter letters. Document more aggressively. Send certified mail every time without exception. When a bureau sends back a verified response, go immediately to the method of verification request under Section 1681i rather than waiting to see if a CFPB complaint produces a different outcome. Do not rely on the regulatory environment to do work that your documentation should be doing. The law is still the law. The statute is still the statute. Build your case on that foundation and the enforcement climate becomes less relevant to your outcome.

Claude is particularly useful in this environment because the rule changes create factual disputes that require specific framing. If your dispute involves a medical debt that should have been covered by the now-vacated CFPB rule, Claude helps you reframe the dispute around the underlying accuracy argument rather than the rule that no longer applies. If your dispute involves a student loan entry from the transition period, Claude helps you frame the furnisher's failure to notify as the accuracy issue rather than treating it as a standard late payment dispute. The facts of your situation have not changed. What changed is which legal hook fits those facts most cleanly in the current environment, and Claude reasons through that translation when you give it the details.

The one constant across every administration and every policy shift is the core FCRA framework. Section 609, Section 611, and Section 623 have not been repealed. The 30 day investigation window has not changed. The requirement to delete unverifiable information has not changed. The prohibition on re-aging has not changed. The seven year reporting window has not changed. Those are your foundation. Everything else is context. Build on the foundation, use the context to sharpen your argument, and let Claude do the translation work between the policy environment and your specific dispute letter. Go to federal609.com and generate your Section 609 request first. What the bureau sends back will show you exactly what version of your information they are holding, which is the only baseline that matters regardless of what any administration has done with the rules around it.

9

What a Derogatory Mark Actually Is: Understanding the Language the Bureaus Use to Describe Your Financial Past Before You Try to Change It

You cannot dispute what you do not understand. Here is the vocabulary the system uses against you.

The word derogatory appears on credit reports, in lender decisions, and in rejection letters, and almost nobody who sees it has ever had it explained to them in plain language. A derogatory mark is any entry on your credit report that indicates you did not meet the terms of a credit agreement. That is the whole definition. It is not a moral judgment. It is not a permanent verdict. It is a data classification that tells lenders you have a history of not paying as agreed, and it triggers a scoring penalty that affects every financial decision you try to make until the entry either falls off naturally or gets removed through a dispute.

The category is broader than most people realize. A single payment that arrived thirty days late is a derogatory mark. A charged-off credit card is a derogatory mark. A collection account for a two hundred dollar medical bill is a derogatory mark. A bankruptcy filing is a derogatory mark. A repossession is a derogatory mark. A foreclosure is a derogatory mark. A settled account, meaning one where you paid less than the full balance as part of a negotiated agreement, is reported as settled for less than full balance which the scoring models treat as derogatory even though you reached an agreement with the creditor. The system treats all of these differently in terms of severity and reporting duration, but they all fall under the same umbrella term and they all drag your score downward.

Understanding the hierarchy of derogatory marks is the first step toward building a rational dispute strategy. Not all negatives hit your score equally. A recent missed payment on an account you otherwise pay on time causes a significant short-term drop but recovers relatively quickly as time passes and you re-establish on-time payments. A charge-off is more serious because it signals to lenders that you stopped paying entirely and the creditor gave up. A collection account on top of a charge-off means the debt was sold and is now being pursued by a third party, which creates two separate derogatory entries for the same original debt. A bankruptcy is the most severe classification in the system, affecting not just your score but your ability to rent an apartment, qualify for a mortgage, or in some cases pass an employment background check.

The scoring models weight recency heavily. A collection account from six years ago carries far less scoring weight than one from six months ago. This is one of the most misunderstood aspects of credit repair. People focus on removing old negatives first because those are the ones that have been bothering them the longest, but the strategic move is almost always to address the most recent derogatory marks first because those are the ones causing the most active damage to your score right now. Claude can help you rank your dispute list by recency and impact before you write the first letter, which means you are not just disputing randomly, you are disputing in the order that produces the fastest measurable improvement.

There is also a distinction worth understanding between derogatory marks that are accurate and those that are not, because the dispute strategy is completely different depending on which category an entry falls into. An accurate derogatory mark, meaning one that correctly reflects something that actually happened, cannot be removed through a dispute based on inaccuracy. The FCRA does not give you the right to delete accurate negative information simply because it hurts your score. What it gives you is the right to have inaccurate, incomplete, or unverifiable information removed. If the mark is accurate, your strategy shifts from dispute to time, credit building, and in some cases goodwill negotiation, which is covered in a later chapter.

An inaccurate derogatory mark is different and that category is far larger than most people expect. The date of first delinquency is wrong. The balance is higher than what you actually owed. The account shows as open when it was closed. The payment history shows a thirty day late in a month when you have a bank statement proving payment. The account belongs to someone with a similar name and was placed on your file by mistake. These are inaccuracies and every single one of them is disputable under federal law. Claude reads account entries and identifies these inconsistencies when you give it the full entry text. It does not guess. It reads the data you give it and flags the fields where something does not add up.

The third category is unverifiable, and this is where the strategy gets interesting. An unverifiable derogatory mark is one that is potentially accurate but cannot be proven through a reasonable investigation because the documentation no longer exists or has been lost through debt sales, system migrations, or the simple passage of time. Old collection accounts are the most common example. A debt from eight years ago that has been sold three times often exists only as a line in a spreadsheet by the time the current collector is reporting it. They cannot produce the original signed agreement. They cannot produce a complete payment history. They cannot prove the balance they are reporting is the correct one. Under the FCRA, if a bureau cannot verify the accuracy of an entry through a reasonable reinvestigation, that entry must be deleted. It does not matter whether the debt was real. It matters whether it can be proven to the legal standard the statute requires.

This is why understanding what derogatory actually means before you start disputing changes everything about your approach. You are not fighting a moral battle about whether you owe money. You are engaging a legal process about whether the information reported about you meets the accuracy and verifiability standards the FCRA requires. That reframe is what separates people who dispute effectively from people who send angry letters and get nowhere. The bureaus do not respond to emotion. They respond to statute citations and documented inconsistencies, and Claude helps you produce exactly that.

Pull your reports from AnnualCreditReport.com, list every derogatory entry, and bring that list to a Claude session before you write a single letter. The analysis comes first. The letters follow from the analysis.

10

Medical Debt and Your Credit Report in 2026 and 2027: What the New Trump Rules Actually Changed, What Got Struck Down, and How to Dispute the Bills That Should Not Be There

The most common source of surprise debt in America is also the most disputable. Here is why.

Medical debt is different from every other category of negative information on a credit report and understanding why it is different is the first step toward understanding how to fight it. You did not choose to get sick. You did not sign a credit application at the emergency room the way you sign one at a car dealership. You were handed a bill after the fact, often without a clear explanation of what the insurance covered, what the provider billed, or what the actual negotiated rate between the provider and your insurer was supposed to be. The debt appears on your credit report and damages your ability to borrow money, rent an apartment, or pass a background check, and in many cases the amount being reported is not even accurate because medical billing errors are extraordinarily common and rarely caught by the people being billed.

The CFPB released research showing that medical debt is a poor predictor of whether a borrower will repay other types of credit obligations, which is the fundamental argument for why it should not be weighted the same way as a missed car payment or a defaulted credit card. The three major credit scoring companies, FICO, VantageScore, and the bureaus themselves, have responded to this research in different ways and at different speeds. VantageScore 4.0 already excludes paid medical debt from its calculations. FICO 10 significantly reduced the weight of medical debt in its scoring algorithm. But lenders do not all use the same scoring model and many still use older versions of FICO that treat medical debt the same as any other collection account. The result is a patchwork where the same medical collection might barely affect your score with one lender and disqualify you with another depending entirely on which model they pull.

The regulatory picture got complicated in 2025 when the CFPB under the previous administration finalized a rule that would have removed medical debt from credit reports entirely and prohibited bureaus from using it as a factor in lending decisions. That rule was challenged in federal court and vacated before it could fully take effect. The practical consequence is that consumers who were waiting for their medical debt to disappear automatically are still waiting for something that is not coming, at least not through that regulatory pathway. What remains is the existing legal framework, which still gives you significant tools to challenge medical debt entries that are inaccurate, unverifiable, or reported in violation of the rules that do still apply.

The first thing to understand about medical debt on credit reports is the timing rules. Medical debt cannot be reported to the bureaus until at least 180 days after the date of service. That six month window is designed to give insurance companies and consumers time to resolve billing disputes before the debt becomes a credit reporting event. If a medical debt appears on your report before the 180 day window has passed, that is an FCRA violation and the entry is disputable on that basis alone regardless of whether you owe the money. Claude can calculate the 180 day window for you if you give it the date of service and the date the entry first appeared on your report. If those dates tell a story that does not add up, Claude writes the dispute letter around that specific timing violation.

The second thing to understand is that medical billing errors are pervasive at a scale that most people find difficult to believe until they look at their own bills closely. Studies of hospital billing consistently find error rates between 30 and 80 percent depending on the complexity of the services and the billing system used by the provider. These errors include charges for services not rendered, duplicate charges for the same service, incorrect procedure codes that trigger a higher charge than the service warrants, failure to apply negotiated insurance rates, and balance billing, which is when a provider bills you for the difference between their charge and what your insurance paid even when they are in-network and legally prohibited from doing so in many states. Any of these errors, if they resulted in a bill that inflated the amount you were reported as owing, gives you grounds to dispute not just with the bureau but directly with the medical provider as a furnisher under Section 623.

When medical debt is sold to a collection agency, a new layer of complexity and a new set of dispute opportunities emerge. The collection agency typically purchases a portfolio of debts for pennies on the dollar and has very limited documentation about the original services, the billing history, or the insurance payments that may have reduced the original balance. What they have is a name, an amount, and a date. What they do not have is the Explanation of Benefits from your insurance company, the itemized bill from the provider, or any documentation that the amount they are reporting accurately reflects what you actually owe after insurance adjustments. When you send a debt validation letter to a medical debt collector demanding they prove the amount and their right to collect it, they frequently cannot produce that documentation. An unverifiable medical collection is subject to mandatory deletion under the same FCRA standard that applies to any other unverifiable entry.

Claude is particularly effective at handling medical debt disputes because the dispute arguments are often highly specific and require careful framing. A letter that simply says this medical bill is wrong will be verified with a two minute automated response. A letter that says this entry reports a balance of three thousand four hundred dollars but the Explanation of Benefits from my insurance company dated June 2024 shows that my maximum patient responsibility after insurance adjustments was one thousand two hundred dollars, meaning the reported balance exceeds my actual obligation by two thousand two hundred dollars, creates a factual dispute that an automated system cannot resolve. Claude helps you build that argument from the documents you have. Give Claude your Explanation of Benefits, your itemized bill if you have it, and the account entry from your credit report. Ask Claude to identify every discrepancy between what the provider billed, what your insurance paid, and what is being reported. Then ask Claude to write the dispute letter around the largest and most documentable discrepancy.

Medical debt also intersects with state law in ways that create additional dispute opportunities depending on where you live. Several states have passed laws that go further than the vacated federal rule by prohibiting medical debt from being reported to credit bureaus or used in lending decisions within their borders. California, Colorado, New York, and several other states have various forms of medical debt credit reporting protections that may apply to your situation. Claude can tell you what your state currently provides in terms of medical debt credit reporting protections if you give it your state of residence, though you should always verify current state law directly given how quickly this area is changing. If your state prohibits reporting of medical debt and a bureau is reporting it anyway, that is both a state law violation and potentially a federal FCRA violation, and the dispute letter cites both.

The emotional weight of medical debt is heavier than almost any other category of negative credit information because the circumstances that created it were usually outside your control. An illness, an accident, a surgery, a hospitalization, none of these are financial decisions in the way that taking out a car loan or opening a credit card is a financial decision. That weight is real and it is valid. But the legal argument does not run on emotion and Claude does not either, which is why the combination works. You bring the facts of what happened. Claude builds the argument from those facts. The argument cites statute, identifies the specific inaccuracy or timing violation, demands documentation the collector likely cannot produce, and positions the entry for deletion.

Go to federal609.com after you complete your medical debt analysis with Claude. The Federal 609 app generates the dispute letters you need for medical collection accounts the same way it generates them for any other negative entry. Your first letter is free. The medical debt that has been sitting on your report since that emergency room visit three years ago is not a life sentence. It is a data entry that has not been properly challenged yet.

11

Student Loans, Federal Debt, and the Credit Report Entries That Almost Nobody Disputes Because They Think They Cannot: What You Can Actually Challenge and What Claude Does With the Information You Give It

Federal debt feels permanent. Some of it is not. Here is the difference.

There is a belief that runs through almost every conversation about student loans and credit repair and it goes something like this: federal debt is untouchable. You cannot dispute a student loan. You cannot remove a federal entry. The government put it there and the government can keep it there as long as it wants. This belief is wrong in ways that matter and understanding exactly where it is wrong is the difference between leaving legitimate dispute opportunities on the table and using every tool the law gives you.

What is true is that a legitimately reported, accurately recorded federal student loan cannot be removed from your credit report simply because you want it gone or because it is hurting your score. The FCRA does not give you the right to delete accurate information. A student loan that you took out, that you defaulted on, and that is being reported accurately with the correct dates and balances is going to stay on your report for seven years from the date of first delinquency regardless of how many letters you send. That part of the belief is accurate.

What is not true is that student loan entries are immune from dispute when they contain errors, and student loan entries contain errors at a rate that should alarm everyone who has ever borrowed for education. The student loan servicing industry has been one of the most consistently criticized sectors of consumer finance for the past two decades, not because of political bias but because the documented record of servicer failures is extensive and well sourced. The Consumer Financial Protection Bureau has published multiple reports detailing how servicers misapplied payments, lost paperwork, placed borrowers in the wrong repayment plans, failed to process income-driven repayment applications, and reported inaccurate information to credit bureaus as a result of their own internal errors. The Department of Education's own Inspector General has documented servicing failures that resulted in borrowers being incorrectly reported as delinquent when they were not. These are not fringe cases. They are documented patterns that created real credit damage for real borrowers who did everything right on their end.

The categories of legitimate student loan disputes are more varied than most people realize. Servicer transfer errors are among the most common. When a loan moves from one servicer to another, which has happened repeatedly across the federal student loan system over the past several years as the Department of Education shifted servicing contracts, payment histories can be reported incorrectly during the transition. A payment you made to the old servicer may not have been properly credited by the new servicer. A period where your account was in administrative hold during the transfer may have been reported as delinquent. These are furnisher accuracy errors and they are disputable under Section 623 directly with the servicer and under Section 611 with the bureaus simultaneously.

Forbearance and deferment reporting errors are another significant category. During the COVID-19 payment pause, which ran from March 2020 through various end dates depending on loan type and administrative decisions, borrowers were supposed to have their accounts reported as current regardless of whether payments were being made. Many servicers did not handle this correctly. Some reported accounts as delinquent during periods when the pause was in effect. Some reported incorrect payment statuses during the restart period when borrowers were resuming payments after years of pause. If your credit report shows negative marks during a period when your loans were supposed to be in a federally mandated pause, that is a direct inaccuracy that Claude can help you frame as a dispute against the servicer as a furnisher and against each bureau reporting the incorrect status.

Income-driven repayment plan errors deserve their own attention because they create a specific type of credit confusion that is difficult to untangle without understanding how these plans work. Under income-driven repayment, your monthly payment is calculated based on your income and family size and can legally be as low as zero dollars per month. A zero dollar payment made under an income-driven repayment plan is a payment made as agreed. It is not a missed payment. It is not a deferment. It is a plan payment that the servicer set at zero based on your income documentation. Some servicers have incorrectly reported these zero dollar payment periods as non-payment or delinquency, creating negative entries for borrowers who were technically current on their loans. If you were enrolled in an income-driven repayment plan and your credit report shows negative marks during that enrollment period, pull your servicer records, confirm your enrollment dates, and bring both the enrollment confirmation and the credit report entry to a Claude session. Claude will identify the discrepancy and write the dispute letter around it.

The restart period after the COVID payment pause ended created its own wave of credit reporting problems that are still working through the system as of 2026. Millions of borrowers resumed payments after a pause that lasted more than three years in some cases. Servicer systems were overwhelmed. Billing statements went out late or not at all. Automatic payment setups that had been suspended during the pause did not automatically restart. Borrowers who thought their automatic payments would resume found out months later, sometimes through a credit report check, that their loans had been reported as delinquent during the restart period because the automatic payment they set up years earlier had been cancelled during the pause and never reactivated. These restart period entries are factual disputes grounded in servicer failure to properly communicate the resumption of payment obligations, and Claude helps you frame that argument with the specificity a Section 611 reinvestigation requires.

Private student loans operate under a different framework than federal loans and offer different dispute possibilities. Private student loans are not subject to federal servicer oversight the way federal loans are, which means the documentation standards and the likelihood of servicing errors vary widely depending on the lender. Private student loans also have statutes of limitations that vary by state, which means a very old private student loan debt may be past the point where a collector can legally sue you to collect it even if it is still within the seven year credit reporting window. Claude can explain how your state's statute of limitations interacts with the credit reporting window for private student loans if you give it your state of residence and the approximate date of first delinquency. Understanding the difference between what a collector can report and what a collector can legally sue you to collect is foundational knowledge that changes how you respond to collection activity on old private student debt.

SBA loans and other federally backed business loans introduce a different complexity because they sit at the intersection of business credit and personal credit in a way that confuses almost everyone who encounters them. An SBA loan that you personally guaranteed does not stay neatly on your business credit profile. Your personal guarantee means that if the business fails to pay, you are personally liable, and that personal liability can appear on your personal credit report depending on the loan type, the default status, and how the SBA or its servicing partners handle the reporting. EIDL loans from the COVID era created a particular version of this problem because many small business owners took out these loans without fully understanding that a personal guarantee attached at certain loan thresholds would eventually surface in their personal credit files if the business struggled. If you have an EIDL or SBA entry on your personal credit report and you believe it is being reported inaccurately, the dispute process is more complex than a standard consumer debt dispute but it follows the same statutory framework. Claude can help you analyze the entry and identify whether the dispute argument runs through the SBA itself, through the servicing partner, or through the bureaus based on what the entry actually shows.

The broader point that connects all of these categories is that federal and government-adjacent debt feels immovable until you look at the specific entry on your specific credit report with specific attention to whether the information as reported is accurate. The loan existing is not the question. The question is whether the dates, balances, payment statuses, and account information recorded by the servicer and transmitted to the bureaus accurately reflect what actually happened in your account history. Servicers make mistakes. Servicing transfers create errors. Payment pauses create reporting complexity. Income-driven plans create confusion about what current means. Every one of those friction points is a potential dispute opportunity if the error produced an inaccurate entry on your report. Bring your student loan credit report entries and your servicer payment history to Claude.

Give Claude both documents. Ask Claude to identify every place where the credit report entry does not match the servicer record. Start the dispute from the largest and most recent discrepancy. The clock is running on these entries the same way it runs on every other negative item, and every month you wait is a month that damage continues that does not have to.

12

Collections, Charge-Offs, and the Debt Sale Chain: How One Unpaid Bill Becomes Three Credit Report Entries and What Claude Does to Untangle Them

The original creditor gave up. Then they sold the problem. Here is what that actually means for your credit file.

A single unpaid debt can generate more negative credit report entries than most people realize, and understanding the chain of events that produces those entries is essential before you can dispute them effectively. It starts with a missed payment. The original creditor, the bank, the credit card company, the medical provider, the auto lender, whoever extended the credit, continues to report the account as delinquent through the normal payment status codes for a period of time. Thirty days late. Sixty days late. Ninety days late. One hundred and twenty days late. Each of those status updates is a separate derogatory notation in your payment history and each one carries scoring weight. By the time the account reaches the charge-off stage, which typically happens between 120 and 180 days of non-payment depending on the creditor's internal policy, the payment history section of that account entry already looks like a documented record of progressive failure.

The charge-off itself is a separate derogatory notation layered on top of the payment history. A charge-off does not mean the debt is forgiven or cancelled. It means the original creditor has written the account off as a loss on their internal books for accounting purposes. They are no longer carrying it as an asset. But the debt still legally exists and you still legally owe it. The charge-off notation tells every lender who pulls your credit report that this creditor decided you were not worth continuing to pursue through normal channels, which is one of the most damaging signals a credit file can contain because it communicates something more serious than a missed payment. It communicates abandonment.

After the charge-off, the original creditor has two options. They can continue to attempt collection internally, which most large creditors do not do because it is expensive and they have already absorbed the accounting loss, or they can sell the debt to a third party debt buyer. Most charge-offs end up sold. The sale price is typically a small fraction of the face value of the debt, sometimes as low as a few cents per dollar of balance, because the debt buyer is purchasing a portfolio of distressed accounts in bulk and pricing in the likelihood that many of them will never be collected. The debt buyer now owns the account and has the legal right to attempt collection and to report the account to the credit bureaus as a collection account.

This is where your credit report goes from one negative entry to two, and sometimes three. The original creditor's charge-off entry remains on your report. That entry belongs to the original creditor and they continue to report it until it reaches the seven year mark and ages off naturally. Simultaneously, the debt buyer who purchased the account opens a new collection account entry on your report reflecting the amount they are attempting to collect. That is a second entry for the same debt. If the first debt buyer is unable to collect and sells the account again to a second collector, which happens frequently with older or harder to collect debts, that second collector may also open a new collection entry on your report. Three entries. One original debt. This is legal under the current credit reporting framework as long as all entries reflect the same original date of first delinquency, which is the critical point and the source of one of the most common errors in collection account reporting.

The date of first delinquency must be consistent across every entry related to the same original debt. The original creditor's charge-off entry should reflect the date you first missed a payment and never caught up. The first collector's entry should reflect that same date. The second collector's entry should reflect that same date. Every entry on your report tied to the same original debt runs the same seven year clock from that single original date. What collectors frequently do, either through error or intentional manipulation, is report a newer date of first delinquency that restarts the clock and keeps the entry on your report longer than the law allows. This practice, called re-aging, is an FCRA violation. It is also one of the most disputable conditions in all of credit repair because when you can show that three entries for the same debt report three different dates of first delinquency, all three entries become suspect simultaneously.

Claude is exceptionally good at catching re-aging because the analysis is mathematical and Claude does not get tired or distracted doing it. Paste every entry related to the same original debt into a single Claude session. Tell Claude the name of the original creditor, the approximate date you first missed a payment, and the current status of each entry as reported. Ask Claude to identify every date of first delinquency shown across the entries and tell you whether they are consistent with each other and whether they are consistent with the seven year reporting window. If Claude finds inconsistencies, it tells you which entry has the most legally vulnerable date and writes the dispute argument around that specific number. A dispute that says this collection entry reports a date of first delinquency that is eighteen months more recent than the date reported by the original creditor for the same account, and this inconsistency indicates re-aging in violation of 15 U.S.C. Section 1681c, is a dispute that is extremely difficult for a collector to survive a reinvestigation with.

The debt validation angle is equally powerful for collection accounts and it works in parallel with the bureau dispute rather than sequentially. When you send a debt validation letter to the collector under FDCPA Section 1692g, you are demanding that they prove the debt is yours, the amount is correct, and they have the legal right to collect it. Collection agencies that purchased debt through multiple sales often cannot produce this documentation. What they bought was a spreadsheet. The chain of custody documents proving the debt was legitimately assigned from the original creditor through every subsequent sale is frequently incomplete or entirely absent. Without that documentation, the collector cannot legally continue collection activity and the entry on your credit report becomes unverifiable, which means it must be deleted from the bureau's file if they cannot verify it through a reasonable reinvestigation.

The practical workflow for a collection account dispute runs through three channels at the same time. The debt validation letter goes to the collector via certified mail demanding proof of the debt and the chain of ownership. The Section 611 reinvestigation demand goes to each bureau reporting the collection entry, citing the specific date inconsistency or inaccuracy you identified with Claude's help. The Section 623 furnisher dispute goes to the collector as well, specifically demanding they investigate the accuracy of every field they are reporting and correct or delete anything that cannot be verified against original documentation. Three letters. Three legal obligations. Three 30 day clocks running simultaneously. This is the dispute stack and it is the most powerful version of the process available to a consumer acting without an attorney.

What happens next depends on how old the debt is, how many times it has been sold, and how well the current collector has maintained their records. For recent debts sold once to a well-organized collection agency, you may receive a validation response that satisfies the legal requirement and a bureau investigation that comes back verified. That is not the end of the process. It is the beginning of the escalation track covered in later chapters. For older debts that have been sold multiple times and live in the portfolios of smaller or less organized collectors, the response to a well-crafted dispute stack is frequently silence, a deletion notice, or a partial response that creates new grounds for escalation. Either way, you are moving forward. Either way, Claude helped you build the argument. And either way, the entry that has been sitting on your report costing you points and costing you opportunities is closer to coming off than it was before you sent the first letter.

13

Bankruptcy and Your Credit Report: What Filing Actually Does to Your File, How Long It Stays, What You Can Dispute Inside a Bankruptcy Record, and How to Rebuild From the Day the Discharge Is Signed

Bankruptcy is not the end of your credit story. It is a legal tool that millions of Americans have used and recovered from. Here is what it actually does to your file.

The word bankruptcy carries more psychological weight than almost any other term in personal finance. People avoid it when they should consider it, delay it when it would help them, and feel shame about it long after the legal process is complete. That shame is not useful and this chapter is not going to reinforce it. Bankruptcy is a legal mechanism built into the federal code specifically because Congress recognized that people encounter financial situations they cannot resolve through ordinary means, and that a functioning economy requires a structured way for individuals and businesses to reset when debt becomes mathematically impossible to resolve. The law exists because the situation it addresses is real and common. Understanding what bankruptcy actually does to your credit file, as opposed to what people fear it does, is the starting point for using the post-bankruptcy period effectively.

There are two forms of personal bankruptcy that most consumers encounter. Chapter 7 is a liquidation bankruptcy. In a Chapter 7 case, most of your unsecured debts, meaning credit cards, medical bills, personal loans, and similar obligations, are discharged entirely. Discharged means legally eliminated. You no longer owe them. The creditors can no longer legally collect them. The process typically takes three to six months from filing to discharge. Not all debts are dischargeable in Chapter 7. Student loans are almost never discharged except in cases of extreme hardship that meet a very high legal standard. Child support and alimony cannot be discharged. Most tax debt cannot be discharged though there are exceptions for older tax liabilities that meet specific criteria. Criminal fines and restitution cannot be discharged. But the bulk of what most people carry as consumer debt, the credit cards, the medical bills, the personal loans, the payday loans, can be eliminated through a Chapter 7 discharge.

Chapter 13 is a reorganization bankruptcy rather than a liquidation. Instead of eliminating debt outright, Chapter 13 creates a court-supervised repayment plan that runs three to five years during which you make monthly payments to a trustee who distributes funds to your creditors according to the plan. At the end of the plan, remaining eligible dischargeable debt is eliminated. Chapter 13 is often used by people who have assets they want to protect, most commonly a home where they have fallen behind on mortgage payments, because Chapter 13 allows you to cure mortgage arrears through the repayment plan in a way that Chapter 7 does not. Chapter 13 is also used by people whose income exceeds the means test threshold for Chapter 7, which requires that your income fall below a certain level relative to your state's median income to qualify for immediate liquidation.

On your credit report, a Chapter 7 bankruptcy appears as a public record and remains reportable for ten years from the date of filing. A Chapter 13 bankruptcy remains reportable for seven years from the date of filing. These are the maximum reporting windows under the FCRA. The accounts included in the bankruptcy, the individual credit cards, medical debts, and other discharged obligations, remain on your report for seven years from the date of first delinquency on each individual account, which is typically before the bankruptcy filing date. This means that in practice, many of the individual accounts included in a bankruptcy begin aging off your report before the bankruptcy public record itself disappears, and your credit profile starts recovering from the bottom up even while the bankruptcy notation is still present.

The post-discharge credit reporting errors that people encounter are numerous and well documented. The most common is a creditor continuing to report a balance or a collection status on an account that was included in and discharged by the bankruptcy. Once a debt is discharged, the creditor is legally prohibited from attempting to collect it or from reporting it as an active debt with a balance owed. An account that shows a balance after a bankruptcy discharge is a violation of the discharge injunction, which is a federal court order. It is also an FCRA inaccuracy because reporting a balance on a legally eliminated debt is factually false. This is one of the strongest dispute arguments in all of credit repair because you have a federal court document, the discharge order, that directly contradicts what the creditor is reporting.

Claude handles post-bankruptcy disputes effectively because the argument is straightforward when you have the right documentation. You give Claude your bankruptcy discharge date, your case number, and the credit report entry showing the account with a post-discharge balance. You ask Claude to write a dispute letter citing the discharge, the federal case number, the date the discharge was entered, and the specific FCRA provision requiring accurate reporting. The letter goes to the bureau as a Section 611 dispute and simultaneously to the creditor as a Section 623 furnisher dispute. Creditors rarely fight these because the discharge order is a federal court document and contesting it exposes them to sanctions for violating the discharge injunction, which is a separate federal legal proceeding entirely apart from the FCRA dispute process.

The second most common post-bankruptcy credit reporting error involves accounts that were included in the bankruptcy being reported with incorrect dates. The date of first delinquency should reflect when the account first went past due, which predates the bankruptcy filing. Some creditors update the date to the bankruptcy filing date or the discharge date, which restarts the seven year reporting clock and keeps the entry on your report longer than it should legally appear. Others fail to update the account status to reflect that the debt was discharged, leaving it showing as charged off or in collections with an active balance when the legal reality is that the debt no longer exists. Each of these is a separate dispute opportunity and Claude identifies them when you paste the account entries into a session alongside your discharge documentation.

The rebuild that happens after bankruptcy is real and it happens faster than most people who have just filed expect. The credit scoring models respond to positive new information added to your file regardless of what is already there from the past. A secured credit card opened the month after discharge, used for small regular purchases, and paid in full every month before the statement closes starts adding positive payment history immediately. That positive history accumulates. Your score begins moving upward. The bankruptcy notation is still present but its relative weight in the scoring calculation diminishes as the proportion of recent positive information grows. Within twelve to eighteen months of a discharge, many people who file Chapter 7 reach credit scores in the 620 to 650 range, which is enough to qualify for certain auto loans and some credit products. Within three to four years, with consistent positive behavior, scores in the 700 range are achievable for many filers even with the bankruptcy still present on the report.

Claude is useful throughout the rebuild period, not just for disputes. Ask Claude to build you a month by month credit rebuild plan starting from your discharge date. Give Claude your current score if you know it, the accounts that were discharged, and any credit accounts that survived the bankruptcy intact. Ask Claude what to open first, what credit limits to target, what utilization to maintain, and what the realistic score trajectory looks like over the next 24 months given your specific starting point. Claude does not have access to your live credit file but it reasons from the information you give it and produces a plan that is specific to your situation rather than generic advice that could apply to anyone. The plan Claude builds becomes your operating document for the rebuild. Federal 609 supports the dispute side of the post-bankruptcy process. Your secured card and your discipline support the build side. Both run simultaneously from day one after discharge and the combination is how people come out of bankruptcy stronger than they went in, which happens more often than the cultural narrative around bankruptcy allows people to believe.

14

Bankruptcy and Your Credit Report: What Filing Actually Does to Your File, How Long It Stays, What You Can Dispute Inside a Bankruptcy Record, and How to Rebuild From the Day the Discharge Is Signed

Bankruptcy is not the end of your credit story. It is a legal tool that millions of Americans have used and recovered from. Here is what it actually does to your file.

The word bankruptcy carries more psychological weight than almost any other term in personal finance. People avoid it when they should consider it, delay it when it would help them, and feel shame about it long after the legal process is complete. That shame is not useful and this chapter is not going to reinforce it. Bankruptcy is a legal mechanism built into the federal code specifically because Congress recognized that people encounter financial situations they cannot resolve through ordinary means, and that a functioning economy requires a structured way for individuals and businesses to reset when debt becomes mathematically impossible to resolve. The law exists because the situation it addresses is real and common. Understanding what bankruptcy actually does to your credit file, as opposed to what people fear it does, is the starting point for using the post-bankruptcy period effectively.

There are two forms of personal bankruptcy that most consumers encounter. Chapter 7 is a liquidation bankruptcy. In a Chapter 7 case, most of your unsecured debts, meaning credit cards, medical bills, personal loans, and similar obligations, are discharged entirely. Discharged means legally eliminated. You no longer owe them. The creditors can no longer legally collect them. The process typically takes three to six months from filing to discharge. Not all debts are dischargeable in Chapter 7. Student loans are almost never discharged except in cases of extreme hardship that meet a very high legal standard. Child support and alimony cannot be discharged. Most tax debt cannot be discharged though there are exceptions for older tax liabilities that meet specific criteria. Criminal fines and restitution cannot be discharged. But the bulk of what most people carry as consumer debt, the credit cards, the medical bills, the personal loans, the payday loans, can be eliminated through a Chapter 7 discharge.

Chapter 13 is a reorganization bankruptcy rather than a liquidation. Instead of eliminating debt outright, Chapter 13 creates a court-supervised repayment plan that runs three to five years during which you make monthly payments to a trustee who distributes funds to your creditors according to the plan. At the end of the plan, remaining eligible dischargeable debt is eliminated. Chapter 13 is often used by people who have assets they want to protect, most commonly a home where they have fallen behind on mortgage payments, because Chapter 13 allows you to cure mortgage arrears through the repayment plan in a way that Chapter 7 does not. Chapter 13 is also used by people whose income exceeds the means test threshold for Chapter 7, which requires that your income fall below a certain level relative to your state's median income to qualify for immediate liquidation.

On your credit report, a Chapter 7 bankruptcy appears as a public record and remains reportable for ten years from the date of filing. A Chapter 13 bankruptcy remains reportable for seven years from the date of filing. These are the maximum reporting windows under the FCRA. The accounts included in the bankruptcy, the individual credit cards, medical debts, and other discharged obligations, remain on your report for seven years from the date of first delinquency on each individual account, which is typically before the bankruptcy filing date. This means that in practice, many of the individual accounts included in a bankruptcy begin aging off your report before the bankruptcy public record itself disappears, and your credit profile starts recovering from the bottom up even while the bankruptcy notation is still present.

The post-discharge credit reporting errors that people encounter are numerous and well documented. The most common is a creditor continuing to report a balance or a collection status on an account that was included in and discharged by the bankruptcy. Once a debt is discharged, the creditor is legally prohibited from attempting to collect it or from reporting it as an active debt with a balance owed. An account that shows a balance after a bankruptcy discharge is a violation of the discharge injunction, which is a federal court order. It is also an FCRA inaccuracy because reporting a balance on a legally eliminated debt is factually false. This is one of the strongest dispute arguments in all of credit repair because you have a federal court document, the discharge order, that directly contradicts what the creditor is reporting.

Claude handles post-bankruptcy disputes effectively because the argument is straightforward when you have the right documentation. You give Claude your bankruptcy discharge date, your case number, and the credit report entry showing the account with a post-discharge balance. You ask Claude to write a dispute letter citing the discharge, the federal case number, the date the discharge was entered, and the specific FCRA provision requiring accurate reporting. The letter goes to the bureau as a Section 611 dispute and simultaneously to the creditor as a Section 623 furnisher dispute. Creditors rarely fight these because the discharge order is a federal court document and contesting it exposes them to sanctions for violating the discharge injunction, which is a separate federal legal proceeding entirely apart from the FCRA dispute process.

The second most common post-bankruptcy credit reporting error involves accounts that were included in the bankruptcy being reported with incorrect dates. The date of first delinquency should reflect when the account first went past due, which predates the bankruptcy filing. Some creditors update the date to the bankruptcy filing date or the discharge date, which restarts the seven year reporting clock and keeps the entry on your report longer than it should legally appear. Others fail to update the account status to reflect that the debt was discharged, leaving it showing as charged off or in collections with an active balance when the legal reality is that the debt no longer exists. Each of these is a separate dispute opportunity and Claude identifies them when you paste the account entries into a session alongside your discharge documentation.

The rebuild that happens after bankruptcy is real and it happens faster than most people who have just filed expect. The credit scoring models respond to positive new information added to your file regardless of what is already there from the past. A secured credit card opened the month after discharge, used for small regular purchases, and paid in full every month before the statement closes starts adding positive payment history immediately. That positive history accumulates. Your score begins moving upward. The bankruptcy notation is still present but its relative weight in the scoring calculation diminishes as the proportion of recent positive information grows. Within twelve to eighteen months of a discharge, many people who file Chapter 7 reach credit scores in the 620 to 650 range, which is enough to qualify for certain auto loans and some credit products. Within three to four years, with consistent positive behavior, scores in the 700 range are achievable for many filers even with the bankruptcy still present on the report.

Claude is useful throughout the rebuild period, not just for disputes. Ask Claude to build you a month by month credit rebuild plan starting from your discharge date. Give Claude your current score if you know it, the accounts that were discharged, and any credit accounts that survived the bankruptcy intact. Ask Claude what to open first, what credit limits to target, what utilization to maintain, and what the realistic score trajectory looks like over the next 24 months given your specific starting point. Claude does not have access to your live credit file but it reasons from the information you give it and produces a plan that is specific to your situation rather than generic advice that could apply to anyone. The plan Claude builds becomes your operating document for the rebuild. Federal 609 supports the dispute side of the post-bankruptcy process. Your secured card and your discipline support the build side. Both run simultaneously from day one after discharge and the combination is how people come out of bankruptcy stronger than they went in, which happens more often than the cultural narrative around bankruptcy allows people to believe.

15

Tax Debt, IRS Liens, and What the Government Can and Cannot Put on Your Credit Report: The Distinction Most People Get Completely Wrong

Most tax debt stopped appearing on credit reports years ago. What still shows up is worth understanding precisely.

In 2017 the three major credit bureaus quietly made one of the most consumer-friendly changes in modern credit reporting history and almost nobody noticed. Equifax, Experian, and TransUnion simultaneously stopped reporting civil judgments and tax liens from their databases as part of a settlement with state attorneys general over data accuracy concerns. The National Consumer Assistance Plan, which drove that change, required the bureaus to remove public record data that did not meet strict standards for matching information to the correct consumer. Tax liens failed that standard in large numbers because IRS lien records frequently lacked sufficient identifying information like Social Security numbers and dates of birth to be matched to a consumer file with confidence. The result was mass removal. Billions of dollars in tax lien records came off credit reports across the country and the people who had those liens on their files saw immediate score improvements without filing a single dispute letter.

What this means practically in 2026 is that a federal tax lien filed by the IRS almost certainly does not appear on your Equifax, Experian, or TransUnion credit report. If you search your report and find no IRS lien entry, that is the expected outcome, not an oversight. The lien may still exist as a public record in county courthouse filings and it may still appear in background checks run by certain lenders, title companies, and employers who search public record databases directly rather than relying on bureau reports. But for purposes of your credit score and the standard credit report a lender pulls when you apply for a mortgage or a car loan, the IRS lien is almost certainly invisible.

The distinction that matters is between what appears on a standard credit report and what appears on a comprehensive background search. If you are applying for a mortgage, the lender will likely conduct a public records search that goes beyond the three bureau reports. IRS tax liens are recorded in the public record at the county level when they are filed and those records are searchable regardless of whether the bureaus include them in your credit file. A lender doing a thorough underwriting review will find a federal tax lien in the public record even if it does not appear on your credit report. Understanding this distinction prevents the unpleasant surprise of assuming your tax situation is invisible to lenders because it does not show on your bureau report.

State tax liens operate under different rules than federal liens and the picture is less uniform. Some states still have their lien data represented in bureau files through data arrangements that predate the 2017 changes. Some states have their lien records accessible through the same public record searches that surface IRS liens. The presence or absence of a state tax lien on your credit report depends on which state you live in, how that state's public record data flows to the bureaus, and whether your specific lien was caught up in the 2017 removals or not. Claude can help you reason through what to expect for your state if you give it the state and the approximate date the lien was filed, though verifying the current status of your specific lien requires pulling your actual reports and in some cases searching your county recorder's records directly.

What does still appear on credit reports related to tax issues is installment agreement payment history when those agreements are reported through a creditor rather than the IRS directly, and state income tax debts that have been assigned to collection agencies in states that permit private collection of state tax obligations. If your state contracted with a private collection agency to pursue your state tax debt, that collection account may appear on your credit report the same way any other collection account does, and it is disputable under the same FCRA framework. The collection agency is a furnisher. The debt validation and Section 623 dispute process applies. Claude builds that letter the same way it builds any other collection dispute letter. The government origin of the underlying debt does not change the dispute mechanics once the debt is in private collection.

The practical takeaway is narrow but important. Check your credit reports before assuming your tax situation has credit consequences, because in most cases for federal tax debt it does not appear the way people fear it will. If you do find a tax-related entry on your report, identify whether it is a federal lien that should have been removed under the 2017 changes, a state lien, or a private collection account for state tax debt, because each of those three scenarios has a different response. Claude helps you identify which category you are dealing with and what the appropriate dispute argument is once you give it the entry text and the underlying facts. The IRS has significant power over your finances but its reach into your credit report is considerably more limited than most people believe, and knowing that distinction is worth more than any generic advice about dealing with tax debt ever will be.

16

How to Rebuild Your Credit Score From Any Starting Point: The Real Mechanics of What Moves the Number and What Wastes Your Time

Your score is not a mystery. It is a formula. Here is what actually goes into it.

The credit score feels personal because the consequences of it are personal. You feel it when the interest rate comes back higher than you expected, when the apartment application gets denied, when the car dealer sends you to the finance office with a look on his face that tells you before he says anything that the terms are not going to be what you hoped. The score feels like a judgment. It is not. It is an output. It is the result of a calculation that runs on the data in your credit file and produces a number that lenders use to predict the probability that you will repay what you borrow. When you understand what goes into the calculation you stop trying to manage the score and start managing the inputs, which is the only approach that produces lasting results.

Payment history is the largest single factor in your score regardless of which scoring model the lender is using. FICO weights it at 35 percent of your total score. VantageScore weights it similarly under the category it calls payment history and depth of credit combined. What this means practically is that no other action you take with your credit file produces the sustained long-term score improvement that consistent on-time payments produce. Not disputing old collections. Not opening new accounts. Not paying down balances in a single month. All of those things matter and some of them matter significantly in the short term, but none of them replace the compounding effect of twelve consecutive on-time payments, then twenty-four, then thirty-six. Every month that passes with every account current adds to a track record that scoring models weight heavily because it is the most reliable signal available that you intend to honor your obligations going forward.

The second factor is credit utilization, which is the ratio of your current revolving balances to your total revolving credit limits across all accounts. If you have three credit cards with a combined limit of ten thousand dollars and you are carrying combined balances of six thousand dollars, your utilization is sixty percent. That is high and it is costing you points every month it stays there. Scoring models respond to utilization in real time, meaning your score reflects your current utilization as reported on your most recent statements rather than some historical average. This makes utilization the fastest lever available to most people in the short term because paying down a balance produces a score improvement within one to two billing cycles, which is faster than almost any other credit action. The target that research consistently supports is keeping total utilization below ten percent if you want to maximize your score. The commonly cited thirty percent threshold is not a target. It is the point below which you stop being actively penalized. Below ten percent is where the scoring benefit is fully realized.

The third factor is the age and depth of your credit history, which includes the average age of all your accounts, the age of your oldest account, and the variety of credit types you have used successfully. This factor is largely outside your direct control in the short term because time is the only thing that ages your accounts. What you can control is what you do not do. Closing old credit card accounts shortens your average account age and can reduce your total available credit simultaneously, both of which hurt your score. People close old accounts thinking they are cleaning up their file and end up watching their score drop for reasons they do not immediately understand. Unless an old account carries an annual fee that outweighs the credit benefit of keeping it open, leave it open and use it occasionally for a small purchase to keep it active. The account age it represents is working in your favor silently every month.

New credit inquiries are the fourth factor and they are the most misunderstood. A hard inquiry, the kind that results from a credit application, drops your score by a small amount, typically five to ten points, for a short period. That drop is temporary and recovers within a few months. The anxiety people feel about hard inquiries often prevents them from applying for credit products that would actually help their rebuild, which is the wrong tradeoff. A secured card that adds twelve months of positive payment history to your file is worth more than the five points you temporarily lost when you applied for it. Rate shopping for a mortgage or an auto loan is handled differently by the scoring models. Multiple hard inquiries for the same loan type within a fourteen to forty-five day window, depending on the scoring model, are counted as a single inquiry because the models recognize that shopping for the best rate on one loan is rational consumer behavior and should not be penalized as if you were applying for multiple new credit lines.

The practical rebuild sequence for someone starting from a low score or a clean slate after bankruptcy or settlement follows a clear order. The first step is a secured credit card from a bank or credit union that reports to all three bureaus. Not all secured cards report to all three and a secured card that only reports to one bureau is producing a third of the benefit it could produce. Use the card for one small recurring purchase each month, something you would buy anyway like a streaming subscription or a gas fill-up, and pay the full balance before the statement closing date. Paying before the closing date means the statement reports a zero or near-zero balance which keeps your utilization low. Paying the minimum and letting a balance carry forward costs you interest and raises your utilization simultaneously. Neither outcome helps your score.

The second step, after three to six months of clean payment history on the secured card, is a credit builder loan from a credit union or community bank. A credit builder loan works differently from a normal loan. Instead of receiving the money upfront, you make monthly payments into a savings account that you cannot access until the loan is paid off. The lender reports your payments to the bureaus each month. At the end of the loan term you receive the money you paid in, minus any fees, and you have added a year or more of installment loan payment history to your credit file. The combination of revolving credit, which is the card, and installment credit, which is the loan, satisfies the credit mix factor and adds payment history across two account types simultaneously.

The third step is patience applied consistently. The rebuild is not a sprint. It is a compounding process that accelerates as the track record grows. Claude is useful throughout this period not for disputes, because the dispute phase should largely be complete before the rebuild phase begins in earnest, but for planning and tracking. Ask Claude to build you a month by month projection based on your starting score, your current accounts, and your plan. Give Claude your utilization targets, your planned payment schedule, and any new accounts you intend to open. Ask Claude to tell you what the score impact of each action is likely to be and in what timeframe. Claude cannot access your live file but it reasons accurately from the inputs you give it and produces a plan that is specific to your situation. The plan keeps you from making the common mistakes that slow the rebuild down, and the mistakes are consistent enough across cases that knowing them in advance is genuinely valuable. Closing old accounts. Applying for too many new accounts at once. Letting utilization creep back up after paying it down. Missing a single payment during the rebuild phase, which resets the most recent payment history and costs disproportionately more than a missed payment would cost someone with a long established positive history. All of these are avoidable with a clear plan and Claude helps you build and maintain that plan from your specific starting point.

17

Business Credit: How It Works as a Separate System, Why It Does Not Automatically Connect to Your Personal File, and How to Dispute Errors in Both Without Confusing the Two

Your business has a credit file that most business owners have never seen. Here is what is in it and what to do when something is wrong.

Most small business owners discover business credit the wrong way. They apply for a business loan or a vendor account and find out that their business has a credit profile they never built intentionally, or they find out their business has no credit profile at all despite years of operation, or they find out that something negative is sitting in their business file from an old account they forgot about or never knew existed. The business credit system operates in parallel to the personal credit system but it follows different rules, uses different bureaus, and produces different reports that are not governed by the same consumer protections that make personal credit disputes possible under the FCRA.

The three major business credit bureaus are Dun and Bradstreet, Equifax Business, and Experian Business. These are separate from the consumer bureaus even when they share a parent company name. A dispute you file with Equifax for your personal credit report has no effect on your Equifax Business report and vice versa. The data in your business file comes from different sources than your personal file and the rules governing how that data is collected, reported, and corrected are substantially different. Business credit reports are not protected by the FCRA because the FCRA is a consumer protection statute that applies to consumer credit, meaning credit extended to individuals for personal, family, or household purposes. Business credit extended to a legal entity, an LLC, a corporation, or a partnership, falls outside the FCRA's jurisdiction in most circumstances.

This distinction matters enormously when something goes wrong in your business credit file. You do not have the same statutory dispute rights that you have for personal credit. There is no mandatory 30 day investigation window backed by federal law. There is no requirement that the bureau delete unverifiable information within a specific timeframe. The dispute process for business credit is governed by each bureau's own internal policies, which means your leverage is different and your strategy needs to account for that difference from the beginning.

Dun and Bradstreet is the dominant player in business credit and the one most vendors and lenders check first when extending net payment terms or business credit lines. Your Dun and Bradstreet file is built around your DUNS number, which is a unique nine digit identifier that D&B assigns to your business. If you have never registered your business with D&B and claimed your DUNS number, your business may have a thin or nonexistent file, or D&B may have created a file from public records and trade payment data that you have never reviewed. Claiming your DUNS number and reviewing your D&B file is the first step for any business owner who wants to understand where their business credit currently stands. D&B allows businesses to dispute inaccurate information directly through their CreditSignal or D&B

Credit products, and the dispute process involves submitting documentation that supports the correction you are requesting.

The most common errors in business credit files fall into categories that are familiar from the personal credit world but arrive through different channels. Payment experiences reported by vendors or suppliers that do not accurately reflect when you actually paid. Public record information like liens or judgments that have been satisfied but still show as outstanding. Basic identifying information errors where your business name, address, or industry classification is wrong, which can cause your file to be confused with another business or can suppress your credit profile from showing up correctly in lender searches. Accounts that belong to a different business with a similar name that have been merged into your file. Each of these requires a different correction approach and the documentation you need varies depending on which bureau holds the error and what their specific correction process requires.

The personal guarantee issue is where business credit and personal credit become genuinely entangled and where confusion creates real financial consequences. When you personally guarantee a business loan or a business credit card, you are agreeing that if the business fails to pay, you will pay from your personal assets. The creditor's legal right to pursue you personally in the event of default is what the guarantee creates. Whether and how that guarantee appears on your personal credit report depends on several factors. If the business account is performing, meaning payments are being made on time, most business accounts with personal guarantees do not appear on your personal credit report because the lender has no reason to invoke the guarantee. If the business account goes delinquent, the lender may begin reporting the account to your personal credit bureaus because they are now treating you as the responsible party under the guarantee. This is when people are surprised to find business debt on their personal credit report and it is exactly the scenario where understanding the intersection of the two systems is essential.

Claude is useful for navigating this intersection because the analysis requires holding multiple variables simultaneously. Give Claude the details of the business account, the personal guarantee terms if you have them, the current payment status, and the entry as it appears on your personal credit report if it is showing there. Ask Claude whether the personal reporting is consistent with the guarantee terms and the account status. Ask Claude what dispute argument applies if the account is being reported to your personal file prematurely or inaccurately. The dispute for a business account incorrectly appearing on your personal file runs through the Section 611 and Section 623 process the same way any other personal credit dispute does, because once a furnisher is reporting to your personal credit file, the FCRA governs that reporting regardless of the underlying nature of the debt.

Building business credit intentionally from the beginning prevents most of these problems. The sequence that works is registering your business as a legal entity, obtaining an EIN from the IRS, opening a dedicated business bank account that is completely separate from your personal finances, and establishing trade lines with vendors who report to the business bureaus. Net 30 accounts with office supply companies, shipping vendors, and business service providers are the starting point because these vendors extend credit without requiring an established business credit history and they report your payment performance to D&B and the business bureaus. Paying these accounts early rather than on time produces the best reporting outcome because D&B's PAYDEX score, which is the primary D&B scoring metric, rewards early payment with a perfect score of 80 and above while on-time payment produces a score of exactly 80. The distinction between early and on time matters more in business credit than it does in personal credit scoring.

The goal of building a strong business credit profile that is entirely separate from your personal credit is financial separation that protects you in both directions. A business with strong independent credit can borrow without triggering a hard inquiry on your personal report. A business financial setback does not automatically damage your personal score if the business accounts were never personally guaranteed and never reported to your personal file. That separation requires intentional construction from the beginning of the business relationship with credit, and it requires maintaining the legal and financial boundaries between your personal finances and your business finances consistently. Commingling personal and business funds, using personal cards for business expenses, or running business revenue through personal accounts all blur the line that credit and legal liability require you to maintain. Claude can walk you through the specific steps to establish that separation based on your business type, your state of incorporation, and your current financial structure if you give it those details. The separation is not complicated but it requires doing it deliberately and doing it early, because rebuilding that wall after it has been broken is significantly harder than building it correctly from the start.

18

Credit Utilization, Credit Limits, and the Strategic Management of the Number That Moves Your Score Faster Than Anything Else

You have more control over this factor than any other. Most people use that control against themselves.

Utilization is the only major credit scoring factor you can change significantly within a single billing cycle. Payment history takes months to build. Account age takes years. Derogatory marks take time and dispute effort to address. But utilization responds immediately to the decisions you make about your balances right now, which makes it the most actionable lever in the entire credit scoring system and the one worth understanding in the most precise terms possible.

The calculation is straightforward. Your total revolving credit utilization is the sum of all your current revolving balances divided by the sum of all your revolving credit limits expressed as a percentage. If you have two credit cards and one store card with combined limits of fifteen thousand dollars and you are carrying combined balances of nine thousand dollars, your utilization is sixty percent and it is costing you a significant number of points every month it stays there. The scoring models do not care how you accumulated those balances. They do not distinguish between a balance that grew from an emergency and one that grew from discretionary spending. They read the ratio and apply the penalty.

What most people do not know is that utilization is calculated both in aggregate across all revolving accounts and on each individual account separately. A single maxed-out card hurts your score even if your overall utilization across all accounts is low. If you have four credit cards each with a five thousand dollar limit and three of them carry zero balances while the fourth is maxed at five thousand dollars, your aggregate utilization is twenty-five percent which sounds manageable, but the individual card utilization on that fourth card is one hundred percent and the scoring models flag it. Paying down the maxed card is more urgent than spreading payments evenly across all four balances, and Claude can confirm this calculation for your specific account mix if you give it your limits and current balances.

The timing of when you pay relative to your statement closing date is a detail that almost nobody who is not actively working on their credit understands and it makes a measurable difference in the score your lender sees. Your credit card issuer reports your balance to the bureaus on your statement closing date, not on your payment due date. These are different dates and the gap between them is where the strategy lives. If your statement closes on the fifteenth of the month and your payment is due on the tenth of the following month, the balance reported to the bureaus is whatever you owed on the fifteenth regardless of whether you pay in full by the tenth. Paying your balance down before the fifteenth means the bureau receives a lower balance report, which means lower utilization, which means a higher score at the moment it is calculated. If you are preparing to apply for a mortgage, a car loan, or any significant credit product, managing the timing of your payments relative to your statement closing dates for the two to three months before the application is one of the highest-return actions you can take with minimal effort.

Credit limit increases are the other side of the utilization equation and they are underused as a strategic tool. If your balance stays the same but your credit limit increases, your utilization ratio drops without you paying a single dollar of additional debt. A card with a two thousand dollar balance and a four thousand dollar limit carries fifty percent utilization. The same two thousand dollar balance on a card with an eight thousand dollar limit carries twenty-five percent utilization. The balance did not change. The ratio changed because the denominator grew. Most major credit card issuers will consider a credit limit increase request after six to twelve months of on-time payments and responsible use. Some issuers extend automatic increases without a request and without a hard inquiry. Others require a formal request that may trigger a hard inquiry, in which case you want to ask explicitly whether the increase request will result in a hard pull before you initiate it. Claude can help you draft the credit limit increase request letter or prepare for the phone call by identifying the specific language that frames the request around your payment history and responsible use rather than your need for more spending capacity. Issuers respond to the former. They are indifferent to the latter.

The discipline side of utilization management is knowing when to say no to credit that is offered to you. The moment your credit starts recovering, the offers arrive. Pre-approved card offers in the mail. Store cards at checkout with a discount incentive. Credit line increases attached to cards you already carry. Balance transfer offers promising zero percent for eighteen months. Not all of these are bad. Some of them are genuinely useful tools at the right moment in a credit rebuild. But each new account also represents a potential new balance, a hard inquiry at opening, and a reduction in your average account age if the new account is younger than your current average. Opening multiple new accounts in a short period signals to scoring models that you may be seeking credit aggressively, which is associated with higher default risk, and the signal depresses your score even if you manage all the new accounts perfectly.

The framework for deciding whether to accept new credit is simpler than the marketing around credit products makes it seem. Ask three questions before saying yes to anything. Does this account serve a specific function in my credit profile that I do not already have covered, such as adding an installment account when I only have revolving credit. Will I be able to pay this balance in full every month or keep it below ten percent utilization without significant effort. Does the benefit of having this account outweigh the short-term score impact of the inquiry and the account age reduction. If the answer to all three is yes, the account probably makes sense. If any answer is no, the default position should be to decline and revisit in six months when your profile may be in a stronger position to absorb the addition.

The long-term view of utilization management is not about keeping balances at zero permanently. It is about understanding the relationship between what you owe, what you have available, and what that ratio communicates to the people making decisions about your financial future. Credit is a tool. Tools work best when you understand what they are for and use them with intention rather than convenience. Claude can model the utilization impact of any financial decision you are considering if you give it your current account balances, limits, and the proposed change. Ask Claude how your score is likely to respond to paying off one specific card versus spreading the same payment across three cards. Ask Claude whether opening a new card to lower your overall utilization makes sense given your current account age. Ask Claude to build you a utilization management calendar for the three months before your next major credit application. The answers are specific to your numbers and your timeline and they cost you nothing to get right before you make a move that costs you points you spent months building.

19

When to Apply for New Credit, When to Wait, and How to Stop the Pattern of Using Debt to Solve Problems That Debt Created

The offer in your mailbox is not an opportunity. It is a test. Here is how to pass it.

There is a moment in every credit rebuild when the momentum starts to feel real. The score crosses a threshold. The secured card gets upgraded to an unsecured product. The pre-approval letters start arriving. The car dealership that turned you away eighteen months ago sends a mailer saying you are pre-qualified. That moment feels like arrival and it is precisely the moment that requires the most discipline, because the same financial behaviors that created the damage in the first place are most likely to resurface when the pressure of a low score is no longer acute enough to keep them in check.

New credit is not inherently dangerous. It is neutral. What determines whether a new account helps or hurts you is the specificity of your reason for opening it, your capacity to manage it without carrying a balance, and where you are in the rebuild arc when the opportunity arrives. A secured card opened three months after a bankruptcy discharge serves a clear purpose in a profile that has nothing positive reporting. A retail store card opened because the checkout clerk offered twenty percent off your purchase serves no strategic purpose and costs you a hard inquiry, a reduction in average account age, and the temptation of an available balance you did not have ten minutes earlier. The difference between those two decisions is not the credit product itself. It is whether you went looking for it or it found you, and whether the reason for opening it is strategic or impulsive.

The credit industry is extraordinarily good at making new credit feel like financial progress. Zero percent APR for eighteen months sounds like free money until the promotional period ends and the deferred interest charges appear. Cash back rewards sound like income until you realize you are spending more than you would have to earn them. Credit limit increases feel like recognition of your improved standing until you notice your balance crept up to meet the new limit within six months. These are not accidents of product design. They are the intended mechanics of products built to generate interest revenue from people who believe they are using the product strategically when they are actually using it the way the issuer needs them to use it to be profitable.

The framework for evaluating any new credit decision starts with your current utilization and payment history because those two factors tell you whether your profile can absorb a new account without disruption. If your utilization is already below ten percent and you have twelve or more months of clean payment history, your profile is stable enough to consider a new account without significant score risk. If your utilization is above twenty percent or your payment history has a gap in the last twelve months, adding a new account introduces complexity your profile does not need and the inquiry cost is harder to recover from because your foundation is not yet strong enough to absorb it efficiently. Wait. Build the foundation first. The offer will come back. They always do.

Timing a credit application to your statement closing dates and your inquiry history matters more than most people account for. Hard inquiries stay on your report for two years and affect your score for approximately twelve months. If you applied for three accounts in the past six months, adding a fourth creates a pattern that scoring models flag as aggressive credit seeking regardless of how well you have managed the accounts you already have. Space your credit applications at least six months apart when possible and twelve months apart when you are building toward a major application like a mortgage. The mortgage underwriter looks at every inquiry in the past twelve months and asks why you needed that credit. The fewer inquiries you have to explain the cleaner the application file and the less room for a lender to find reasons to complicate the approval.

The deeper pattern worth examining honestly is the relationship between financial stress and credit applications. For many people the impulse to apply for new credit is strongest at exactly the moment when new credit is most dangerous, when income is tight, when an unexpected expense has arrived, when the checking account balance is lower than it needs to be to cover the next week comfortably. In that moment a credit card or a personal loan feels like a solution because it provides immediate liquidity. And it does provide liquidity. What it also provides is a new balance that will need to be serviced from the same income that was already insufficient, which means the problem has been deferred but not resolved and the cost of deferring it includes interest charges that make the eventual resolution more expensive.

Claude is useful here not because it can make the decision for you but because it can model the actual cost of the decision you are considering. Tell Claude what you are thinking about opening, what the interest rate is, what balance you are likely to carry, and what your current monthly cash flow looks like. Ask Claude to calculate what this account will actually cost you over twelve months if you carry a balance at the stated rate, and ask Claude to compare that cost to alternatives like negotiating a payment plan directly with whoever you owe, drawing down savings temporarily, or identifying a discretionary expense that could be reduced to cover the gap. The math is not complicated but seeing it laid out specifically for your situation rather than as a generic warning about debt is often what it takes to make the right decision feel as clear as it actually is.

The question of whether you need credit at all after the rebuild is complete is one that personal finance culture rarely asks directly because the industry that produces most personal finance content has a financial interest in your continued participation in the credit system. The honest answer is that you need enough credit history to maintain a functional score for the purposes that actually require one, primarily housing and major purchases like vehicles where financing is genuinely more practical than cash. Beyond those functional requirements, the case for maintaining and expanding credit access is significantly weaker than the marketing around credit products suggests. A person with two credit cards carrying zero balances, paid in full every month, with a mortgage or auto loan reporting clean payment history, has all the credit infrastructure they need for most financial goals. Every additional account beyond that serves the issuer's revenue model more than it serves your financial health. Knowing that and acting on it is not financial deprivation. It is the clarity that comes from understanding what the system is actually for and using exactly as much of it as your life requires.

20

How to Prepare Your Credit for a Mortgage: What Lenders Actually Look at Beyond the Score, How to Read a Tri-Merge Report, and What to Fix Before You Apply

The score gets you in the door. What is inside the file determines whether you leave with a loan.

The mortgage application process exposes your credit file to a level of scrutiny that no other lending decision comes close to matching. A credit card issuer pulls your score and makes a decision in seconds based on an algorithm. A mortgage underwriter pulls a tri-merge report combining all three bureau files into a single document, reads it line by line, asks questions about every derogatory mark regardless of age, calculates your debt-to-income ratio against the specific loan amount you are requesting, and makes a judgment that involves human review at multiple stages of the process. The score is the entry point. Everything else in the file is the conversation that follows.

Understanding what a tri-merge report is and how it differs from the individual bureau reports you have been working with throughout this book is the first adjustment to make when you shift from general credit repair to mortgage preparation. A tri-merge report pulls your Equifax, Experian, and TransUnion files simultaneously and presents them side by side on a single document. The lender uses this combined view to identify the middle score across all three bureaus, not the highest and not the lowest, and that middle score is the one used for qualification purposes on most conventional mortgage products. If your three scores are 680, 702, and 715, the qualifying score for your application is 702. This means that raising your lowest score matters less than raising your middle score, and Claude can help you identify which bureau's file contains the most disputable or improvable information once you know which bureau is producing the lowest number.

The minimum score thresholds for different mortgage products vary and they shift with market conditions, but the general landscape as of 2026 places conventional loans backed by Fannie Mae and Freddie Mac at a minimum of 620 for most programs, with significantly better rate pricing beginning at 740 and above. FHA loans, which are insured by the Federal Housing Administration and designed for first-time buyers and those with lower down payments, have a minimum of 580 for the standard 3.5 percent down payment program and allow scores as low as 500 with a ten percent down payment, though finding a lender willing to originate at the lower threshold is more difficult than the published minimums suggest. VA loans for eligible veterans and active military have no published minimum score requirement at the federal level though individual lenders typically impose their own overlays starting around 580 to 620. USDA loans for rural property purchases similarly have no federal minimum but carry lender overlays in the same range.

The score threshold gets you to the application. What happens inside the underwriting process is where preparation matters most. Underwriters are trained to look at specific patterns that algorithms sometimes miss or weight differently than a human reader would. A series of late payments concentrated in a single period followed by clean history suggests a situational hardship rather than a character issue, and underwriters are sometimes more forgiving of concentrated past problems with a long clean recovery than algorithms are. A pattern of late payments spread irregularly across multiple years with no clear recovery trajectory is more difficult to explain and more difficult to underwrite regardless of the current score. The story your credit file tells is as important as the number it produces, and preparing your file for a mortgage means understanding and being able to articulate that story clearly.

Mortgage lenders also look at factors that do not appear in a standard consumer credit score calculation. Your debt-to-income ratio, which is your total monthly debt obligations divided by your gross monthly income, is evaluated separately from your credit score and it affects your qualification for specific loan amounts more directly than your score does in many cases. A borrower with a 750 score and a 52 percent debt-to-income ratio will struggle to qualify for a conventional loan because conventional guidelines typically cap debt-to-income at 45 percent for standard approvals and 50 percent with compensating factors. Reducing your debt load before applying is sometimes more important than raising your score by another twenty points, and Claude can calculate your current debt-to-income ratio and tell you exactly which accounts to pay down or pay off to bring the ratio within qualifying range for the loan amount you are targeting.

The mortgage-specific dispute timeline requires planning that general credit repair does not. Most mortgage lenders require that all disputes be removed from your credit file before they will issue a final loan approval. An active dispute notation on a credit report tells an automated underwriting system that the file is in a contested state, and many systems will not issue an approval recommendation when dispute flags are present. This means that if you have been actively disputing items on your report, you may need to withdraw those disputes temporarily to get a clean approval, then reopen them after closing. This is a common situation and mortgage professionals who know what they are doing will walk you through it, but understanding it in advance prevents the confusion and delay that happens when a borrower discovers this requirement two weeks before their closing date.

The preparation timeline for a mortgage application ideally starts twelve months before you intend to apply. In the first three months you pull all three reports, complete your dispute campaign with Claude and Federal 609, and identify the middle score and what is holding it below your target threshold. In months four through six you address utilization, request credit limit increases where appropriate, and avoid any new credit applications that would generate hard inquiries. In months seven through nine you verify that disputes have resolved correctly, check that deleted items have not reappeared, and begin reducing installment loan balances where possible to improve your debt-to-income ratio. In months ten through twelve you maintain clean payment history on every account without exception, avoid closing any accounts, make no new credit applications, and pull your reports one final time thirty days before you intend to apply to confirm everything is clean.

Claude is the planning tool for this entire timeline. Give Claude your three current scores, your current monthly debt obligations, your gross monthly income, and the purchase price you are targeting. Ask Claude to calculate your debt-to-income ratio, identify your qualifying score for the loan type you want, tell you the gap between where you are and where you need to be, and build you a month by month action plan for closing that gap before your target application date. The plan Claude produces will be specific to your numbers and your timeline in a way that generic mortgage readiness advice never is. The mortgage you are working toward is not an abstraction. It is a specific loan amount at a specific price point requiring a specific score and a specific debt-to-income ratio, and the plan that gets you there has to be built around those specific numbers. Go to federal609.com and generate any remaining dispute letters before the twelve month clock starts. The dispute campaign closes first. The build phase follows. The application comes last.

That sequence is not negotiable if you want the cleanest possible file on the day an underwriter reads it.

21

The Clean Slate: How to Rebuild Your Financial Life in the First 90 Days After Bankruptcy, Settlement, or a Major Credit Event

The discharge is signed. The settlement is done. The account is closed. Now what you do in the next 90 days determines the next seven years.

The first 90 days after a major credit event are the most important and the most misunderstood period in the entire credit lifecycle. Most people spend them in a kind of financial paralysis, assuming that the damage is done, that the system has categorized them, and that the only option is to wait out the reporting window while time does its slow repair work. That assumption is wrong and the cost of acting on it is real. The credit rebuild does not begin when the negative marks age off. It begins the day after the event closes, and the difference between someone who starts immediately and someone who waits twelve months is not twelve months of recovery time. It is years, because the compounding effect of positive payment history works forward from whenever you start and cannot be backdated.

The first thing to understand about the immediate post-event period is that your credit file is not empty. It is damaged. Those are different conditions that require different responses. An empty file has no history at all and lenders treat it with caution because there is no data to evaluate. A damaged file has negative history but it also has a structure, account entries, payment records, a length of history, and in many cases some accounts that survived the event intact. That surviving structure is the foundation you build on rather than starting from nothing, which means the rebuild is faster than most people expect if they approach it correctly from the beginning.

In the first two weeks after a bankruptcy discharge, a debt settlement, or any major credit resolution, your first action is to pull all three credit reports from AnnualCreditReport.com and read every entry with fresh eyes. The event you just completed changed the legal status of multiple accounts and that change needs to be reflected accurately in your credit file. A bankruptcy discharge should result in every included account being reported as discharged in bankruptcy with a zero balance. A settlement should result in the settled account being reported as settled for less than full balance, which is negative but accurate, rather than as an active collection or an open charge-off. A paid collection should show a zero balance and a paid status. None of these updates happen automatically or instantly and the errors that appear in the immediate post-event period are among the most disputable conditions in credit reporting because you have fresh documentation of the event, the discharge order, the settlement agreement, the payment confirmation, and the discrepancy between that documentation and what the bureau is reporting is immediately visible and immediately actionable.

Bring those entries to Claude within the first two weeks. Give Claude your discharge date or settlement date, the documentation you have, and the credit report entries as they currently appear. Ask Claude to identify every entry that is not accurately reflecting the post-event status and write the dispute letters for each one. These disputes are among the fastest to resolve because the documentation is unambiguous. A discharge order from a federal bankruptcy court is not a document a bureau can easily argue with. Getting these entries corrected early means your file reflects the actual legal reality of your situation rather than a transitional inaccuracy that costs you points every month it persists.

The secured credit card is the first new account you open and you open it within the first 30 to 60 days of the post-event period, not after you feel ready, not after the score reaches a threshold you have set in your head, but now. The score is going to be low. That is expected and it is not a reason to wait. A secured card does not require a good score to obtain because your deposit secures the credit limit and eliminates the lender's risk. What it requires is a bank account to fund the deposit and the discipline to use it correctly from the first billing cycle. Choose a secured card from a bank that reports to all three bureaus, charges a reasonable annual fee or no annual fee, and has a clear upgrade path to an unsecured product after 12 months of responsible use. Use it for one small recurring charge each month. Pay the full balance three to five days before the statement closing date every single month without exception. That one account, managed correctly for 12 months, adds 12 consecutive on-time payments to your file and begins the recovery that feels impossible from where you are standing in the first days after the event.

The credit builder loan is the second account and you open it 60 to 90 days after the secured card, not simultaneously. Opening both at once creates two hard inquiries in the same month and reduces your average account age on two fronts simultaneously. Staggering them 60 days apart spreads the impact and gives the first account time to begin reporting positive history before the second one opens. A credit builder loan from a credit union or community development financial institution adds an installment account to your profile, which is a different account type than revolving credit and satisfies the credit mix factor that scoring models evaluate. The monthly payment goes into a savings account you cannot access until the loan term ends, so you are simultaneously building credit history and building a small cash reserve, which addresses two of the most urgent needs in the immediate post-event period at the same time.

The 90 day budget is the financial structure that makes the credit rebuild possible. It is not complicated and it does not require a spreadsheet if that feels like too much. It requires knowing three numbers. What comes in each month after taxes. What must go out each month for housing, food, transportation, and utilities. What is left after those two numbers are reconciled. That remainder is what you work with, and every dollar of it in the first 90 days has a specific purpose. The secured card payment comes first because a missed payment in the first 90 days of a rebuild sets you back disproportionately. The credit builder loan payment comes second for the same reason. Everything else, every discretionary purchase, every subscription, every social obligation that costs money, gets evaluated against the question of whether it serves the rebuild or delays it.

Claude is the planning tool for this entire 90 day period and beyond. After you have opened your secured card and initiated your credit builder loan, give Claude your complete financial picture. Your monthly income. Your fixed monthly obligations. Your current credit accounts and their balances. The negative entries still on your report and their approximate ages. Ask Claude to build you a month by month plan for the next 12 months that sequences every credit action in the order that produces the maximum score improvement while maintaining the financial stability to execute it consistently. The plan Claude builds is specific to your numbers and your timeline. It tells you when to request your first credit limit increase, when to apply for the second credit card if one is warranted, when to start monitoring your score for the threshold crossings that open new credit opportunities, and when to pull your reports again to verify that the post-event corrections you disputed in the first two weeks have been properly applied.

The clean slate is not a metaphor. It is a real condition that the legal system created when it resolved your debt situation, and it is available to every person who went through that process regardless of how they feel about it emotionally. The credit system does not care how you feel about what happened. It reads the data and produces a score. Feed it better data consistently and it produces a better score consistently. That is the whole mechanism and it responds to anyone who engages it correctly starting from wherever they are. The 90 days that follow a major credit event are not a waiting room. They are the first chapter of the rebuild and the chapter that determines how fast the rest of the story moves.

22

Cash Management, Living Without Debt Dependence, and the Financial Life That Becomes Possible When Credit Is a Tool You Choose Rather Than a System You Survive

Most people fix their credit and then recreate the same conditions that damaged it. Here is how to break that cycle permanently.

There is a version of financial recovery that looks successful from the outside and feels unstable from the inside. The score is back above 700. The secured card has been upgraded. The collection accounts are gone. The mortgage application is approved. And underneath all of it the same relationship with money that created the original damage is still intact, still running, still making the same decisions that will eventually produce the same outcomes. The credit repair worked. The financial behavior did not change. And the rebuild that took three years to complete begins quietly unraveling from the moment the pressure of a low score is no longer acute enough to enforce the discipline that produced the recovery.

Breaking that cycle requires understanding what caused it in the first place, and the cause is almost never what people think it is. Most people who carry significant credit card debt and struggle with recurring financial instability do not have an income problem in the simple sense of not earning enough money. They have a cash flow management problem, which is a different diagnosis with a different solution. A cash flow problem means that money arrives and departs without a structure that directs it toward the obligations and goals that matter most before it gets absorbed by the obligations and impulses that feel most urgent in the moment. The credit card fills the gap between what arrived and what was needed before the next arrival, and the interest charge on that gap is the invisible tax that compounds quietly until the debt load becomes the defining feature of the financial picture.

Cash management is not budgeting in the traditional sense of tracking every purchase in a spreadsheet and feeling guilty about the ones that do not fit a category. That approach works for some people and fails for most because it requires a level of continuous attention that is difficult to sustain alongside the actual demands of a life. What works more broadly and more durably is a simpler system built around directing money at the moment it arrives rather than tracking it after it departs. When income lands in your account, the first allocation goes to the fixed obligations that cannot be negotiated, housing, utilities, transportation, and minimum debt payments if any remain. The second allocation goes to a savings account that is not connected to your checking account and is not easily accessible through a debit card or mobile transfer. The third allocation covers variable necessities, food, personal care, and household supplies. What remains after those three allocations is discretionary and can be spent without guilt or tracking because the obligations and the savings were funded before the discretionary spending began.

The savings allocation is the element most people skip during a credit rebuild because the margin feels too thin to save anything meaningful and the debt feels like the more urgent problem. This is understandable and it is also the decision that leaves people most vulnerable to the next unexpected expense. An unexpected expense without a cash reserve is a credit card charge. A credit card charge without the cash to pay it immediately is a balance that accrues interest. A balance that accrues interest is the beginning of the same cycle that produced the damage you just spent years repairing. The amount of the savings allocation in the early rebuild period does not matter as much as the consistency of it. Twenty-five dollars a month going into a separate account every month without exception builds a habit and builds a buffer, and the buffer is what prevents the next small crisis from becoming the next large debt accumulation.

The question of whether you need credit at all once the rebuild is complete is worth sitting with honestly rather than accepting the cultural assumption that more available credit is always better than less. The functional case for maintaining credit is real and narrow. A mortgage requires credit history. An auto loan is often more practical than a cash purchase for most people's income levels and asset positions. A credit card used strategically and paid in full monthly provides purchase protection, fraud protection, and travel benefits that cash does not. Beyond those functional uses, the case for expanding credit access is significantly weaker than the financial industry's marketing suggests. A person with a paid-off mortgage, a single credit card carrying a zero balance paid in full every month, and a fully funded emergency reserve has all the credit infrastructure their financial life requires. Every additional open credit line beyond that is an opportunity to accumulate debt that does not exist today.

Claude is useful for designing the cash management system that fits your specific income structure and obligation set. Give Claude your monthly take-home income, your fixed monthly obligations, your variable monthly necessities, and your current savings balance. Ask Claude to design a cash flow allocation system that funds your obligations, builds your reserve, and leaves you with a clear discretionary amount without requiring ongoing tracking. Ask Claude what the minimum emergency reserve is for your specific situation given your income stability and your monthly obligation level. Ask Claude to calculate how many months it would take to build that reserve at different savings allocation amounts so you can see the timeline and choose the pace that fits your current capacity. The system Claude builds is not a generic budget template. It is a structure calibrated to your actual numbers that makes the right financial decisions automatic rather than effortful.

The financial life that becomes available after credit repair is complete and cash management is functioning is qualitatively different from the one that existed before, and it is worth describing concretely because most credit repair content stops at the score without addressing what the score was supposed to unlock. A functioning credit profile combined with a cash reserve and a managed cash flow means that financial decisions are made from a position of choice rather than necessity. You choose whether to finance a car purchase or pay cash based on the interest rate and your investment alternatives rather than based on whether you have any other option. You choose whether to use a credit card for a purchase based on the rewards and protection it provides rather than based on whether your checking account balance will cover the alternative. You choose how much house to buy based on what fits your financial plan rather than based on the maximum amount a lender will approve. That shift from necessity to choice is what financial recovery actually means at its most complete expression and it is available to anyone who builds the credit foundation, manages the cash flow, and maintains the discipline to treat credit as a tool they pick up when it serves them and set down when it does not.

23

FICO 10, VantageScore 4.0, and the Trended Data Revolution: Why the Scoring Model Your Lender Uses in 2026 Is Judging Two Years of Your Financial Behavior, Not a Single Snapshot

The old scoring model took a photograph of your credit file. The new one watches the film.

For most of the history of modern credit scoring, the model that determined whether you qualified for a loan and at what interest rate looked at your credit file the way a camera looks at a scene. It captured a single moment. Your balance on the day the report was pulled. Your payment status as of the most recent reporting cycle. Your total available credit at that instant. The model had no interest in the direction you were traveling. It could not tell whether your balance of four thousand dollars was the result of three years of steady paydown from an original balance of twelve thousand, or whether it represented the beginning of an accumulating spiral that started at five hundred dollars eighteen months ago. Both situations produced the same snapshot and the same score, which meant the model was systematically blind to some of the most important information available about how a borrower actually manages credit over time.

FICO 10 and VantageScore 4.0 changed that. Both models incorporate what the industry calls trended data, which is payment and balance information going back 24 months rather than reflecting only the current state of each account. The practical effect of this change is significant and it runs in both directions. A borrower who has been steadily paying down balances over the past two years, even if their current balance is still relatively high, looks meaningfully different to a FICO 10 calculation than they did to FICO 8. The model sees the trajectory and rewards it. Conversely, a borrower who has been slowly accumulating balances over the same period, even if their current utilization is within what looks like a safe range, looks worse to FICO 10 than to older models because the model sees the direction and penalizes it. The snapshot score and the trended score can diverge significantly depending on which of these patterns describes your financial behavior over the past two years.

The mortgage industry's adoption of these newer models is the development that makes this shift immediately relevant to anyone preparing to apply for a home loan. Fannie Mae and Freddie Mac, the government-sponsored enterprises that back the majority of conventional mortgages in the United States, announced the transition to bi-merge reporting using VantageScore 4.0 alongside FICO 10 as part of a broader modernization of the mortgage underwriting process. The timeline for this transition has moved in stages and the practical implementation varies by lender, but the direction is clear and irreversible. The scoring model that will evaluate your mortgage application in 2026 and 2027 is increasingly likely to look at 24 months of your financial behavior rather than a single moment in time. That changes what preparation for a mortgage application actually means.

The specific behaviors that FICO 10 rewards and penalizes through trended data analysis are worth understanding precisely because they differ in important ways from the optimization logic that worked under older models. Consistent balance reduction over time is the behavior the model rewards most directly. Not a single large paydown in the month before the application, which the model can identify as a short term manipulation, but a steady month over month reduction in revolving balances sustained across multiple billing cycles. A borrower who reduces their total credit card balance by two hundred dollars a month for eighteen months demonstrates a pattern of behavior that FICO 10 interprets as financially disciplined in a way that a borrower who paid off the same total amount in a single transaction the month before applying does not. The model is specifically designed to distinguish between these two situations and it does so by reading the 24 month balance history rather than the current balance alone.

Debt shifting, which is the practice of moving balances from one card to another through balance transfers to lower utilization on specific accounts, is another behavior the trended data model identifies and penalizes in ways older models did not. Under FICO 8, a balance transfer that reduced utilization on a high balance card could produce an immediate score improvement even if the total debt remained unchanged. Under FICO 10, the total balance trajectory across all revolving accounts is visible across 24 months and a balance transfer that moves debt without reducing it shows up as exactly what it is, a repositioning rather than a paydown. The model is not fooled by it and the score improvement that older generation borrowers learned to expect from strategic balance transfers is significantly reduced under the newer scoring logic.

The Claude application for trended data optimization is one of the most sophisticated uses of AI in personal finance that is available to a consumer without hiring a financial advisor. Give Claude 24 months of your credit card statement data, either by pasting in the monthly balance from each statement or by describing the approximate balance trajectory on each account over the period. Ask Claude to map the trended data pattern your accounts would show to a FICO 10 model and identify whether the trajectory is positive, negative, or flat. Ask Claude to calculate the optimal paydown sequence for the next six months that would produce the most favorable trended data pattern for a mortgage application at a specific target date. The calculation involves not just which accounts to pay down but in what order and at what monthly rate to produce a trajectory that the trended data model reads as sustained disciplined reduction rather than a last minute correction.

The medical debt dimension of the 2026 scoring environment intersects with trended data in a way that creates a specific opportunity for borrowers who have medical collections on their report. Under the updated credit bureau policies that took effect in 2023 and continued into 2026, paid medical collections are no longer included in credit report data and medical collections under 500 dollars are excluded from reporting entirely. For borrowers preparing for a mortgage application, this means that a category of negative information that would have appeared in a FICO 8 snapshot calculation may not appear in the VantageScore 4.0 or FICO 10 calculation at all, which can produce a meaningful score difference between what an older model produces and what the mortgage lender's newer model produces. Pulling your reports and identifying which medical entries are subject to these exclusions before your application is part of the mortgage preparation process that Claude can help you systematize. Give Claude your medical collection entries with their balances and dates and ask Claude to identify which ones fall under the current exclusion thresholds and whether they should appear in the newer scoring models your lender is likely to use.

The broader implication of the trended data shift is that credit management in 2026 and beyond rewards exactly the behaviors that produce genuine financial health rather than the behaviors that optimize a snapshot metric. Consistent reduction of balances over time. Avoidance of new debt accumulation. Steady payment history without gaps. These are not sophisticated financial strategies. They are the basic mechanics of spending less than you earn and directing the difference toward obligations that compound in your favor rather than against you. The scoring model caught up to the reality that these behaviors are the most reliable predictor of future creditworthiness and built that reality into the calculation. The consumer who understands this and manages their accounts accordingly for 24 months before a major credit application is not gaming a system. They are demonstrating exactly the pattern of behavior the system was designed to reward, and the score they receive reflects that accurately for the first time in the history of consumer credit scoring.

24

The Medical Debt Sweep of 2026: How to Identify Every Medical Collection That Should Be Gone From Your Credit Report and Use Claude to Remove What Remains

Billions of dollars in medical debt that was damaging credit scores a year ago is no longer supposed to be there. Here is how to find what is still showing up on your report and what to do about it.

The credit reporting landscape for medical debt shifted more dramatically between 2023 and 2026 than it had in the previous two decades combined and most consumers have not checked whether their credit report reflects those changes. The three major bureaus, responding to CFPB pressure, research showing that medical debt is a poor predictor of creditworthiness, and the threat of regulatory action, implemented a series of voluntary changes that removed a substantial portion of medical debt from consumer credit files. Paid medical collections disappeared first. Then medical collections under 500 dollars were excluded entirely regardless of payment status. Then the CFPB proposed a rule that would have eliminated medical debt from credit reporting altogether, a rule that was finalized and then vacated by a federal court before it could fully take effect. The result of this sequence is a patchwork of protections that are real and significant but inconsistently applied, which means that medical debt that should not be on your report under current bureau policies may still be there because the removal was not automatic, universal, or perfectly executed across hundreds of millions of consumer files.

The first action is to pull all three reports and locate every medical entry. Medical debt does not always identify itself clearly as medical. A collection account from a company called National Recovery Agency or Capio Partners or Convergent Outsourcing does not announce in the account name that the underlying debt is medical. You need to look at the original creditor field, which appears in most collection account entries and names the entity that originally held the debt before it was sold to the collector. If the original creditor is a hospital, a physician group, an emergency medical provider, a radiology practice, an anesthesiology group, or any other healthcare entity, the account is medical debt regardless of what the collector's name suggests. Make a list of every account where the original creditor is a healthcare provider. That list is your starting point.

For each entry on that list, you need to establish three facts before you decide how to approach it. The reported balance as it appears on your credit report. The current payment status, meaning whether it is paid, unpaid, or in an unknown status because the collector has changed hands. And the date the medical service was provided or the date the debt first went delinquent if you know it, because the timing interacts with both the bureau exclusion policies and the seven year reporting window under the FCRA. Once you have those three facts for each entry, the analysis becomes systematic and Claude executes it quickly when you give it the information in that structured form.

The exclusion framework as it stands in 2026 works as follows. Medical collections that have been paid in full should not appear on your credit report at all under the current bureau policies. If a paid medical collection is still showing on your report, that entry is reportable under the existing voluntary policy commitments the bureaus have made and it is disputable on that basis. The dispute argument is not a complex legal argument about statute violations. It is a straightforward accuracy argument that the entry reflects a paid account that the bureau's own policies exclude from reporting. Send the dispute to the bureau citing the paid status and the bureau's published policy on paid medical collections. Attach proof of payment if you have it. The removal should be straightforward.

Medical collections under 500 dollars that remain unpaid present a different situation. The bureau exclusion for sub-500 dollar medical collections does not require payment. The collection is supposed to be excluded from reporting based on its balance alone. If you have unpaid medical collections under 500 dollars appearing on your report, those entries are inconsistent with current bureau policy regardless of their payment status and they are disputable on that basis. Claude writes this dispute effectively when you give it the entry, the balance, and a statement that you are disputing based on the bureau's stated policy of excluding medical collections below the 500 dollar threshold. The dispute goes to the bureau directly and the argument is simple because the bureau's own policy supports your position without requiring a complex legal argument.

The itemized hospital bill review is a separate process from the credit report dispute and it runs in parallel rather than sequentially. Hospital billing errors occur at rates that should alarm every patient who receives a bill without reviewing it line by line, and the errors consistently run in the hospital's favor rather than the patient's. Charges for services not rendered appear regularly. Duplicate line items for the same procedure are common. Incorrect procedure codes that trigger a higher charge than the service warrants show up frequently in complex bills involving multiple care providers. Balance billing, where an in-network provider bills you for the difference between their charge and the insurance payment even when they are contractually prohibited from doing so, is a documented practice in states that do not have strong surprise billing protections. Each of these errors inflates the amount you were billed and potentially the amount reported to a collection agency, which means the balance appearing on your credit report may be inaccurate at its source before any question of reporting policy applies.

Claude handles itemized bill analysis with a specificity that makes the process accessible to someone without medical billing expertise. The billing codes on a hospital bill, called CPT codes, are publicly documented and their standard charges are published through the federal price transparency requirements that went into effect in 2021 and were strengthened in subsequent years. Give Claude your itemized hospital bill by describing each line item, the CPT code if it is listed, and the amount charged. Ask Claude to identify any line items that appear duplicated, any charges that seem inconsistent with the described service, and any balance billing that may have occurred based on your insurance coverage. Ask Claude to calculate the total amount you should have been billed after insurance adjustments based on the information available. The difference between what you were billed and what Claude calculates you should have been billed is the basis for a formal billing dispute with the hospital's patient billing department, which is a separate process from the credit report dispute but which can reduce or eliminate the underlying debt that produced the credit entry in the first place.

The CFPB complaint system is available as an escalation tool when a bureau or a medical collector fails to respond appropriately to a dispute that is clearly supported by current policy. A bureau that continues to report a paid medical collection after receiving a dispute with proof of payment is not complying with its own stated policy and a CFPB complaint documenting that noncompliance creates an external record that the bureau must respond to within a specific timeframe. Medical debt collectors who continue to attempt collection on debts under 500 dollars that are excluded from bureau reporting under current policy are operating in a gray area that the CFPB has shown interest in, and a formal complaint creates documentation that may support broader action if the pattern is widespread. Claude helps you write CFPB complaints with the same specificity it brings to dispute letters. Give Claude the timeline of your dispute, what you submitted, what the bureau or collector responded with, and what the correct outcome should be based on current policy. Claude structures the complaint around the factual sequence and the policy violation in a way that is more likely to generate a substantive response than a complaint written in general terms about feeling mistreated.

The medical debt sweep of 2026 represents a genuine and significant improvement in the consumer credit reporting environment and it is worth taking the time to verify that your credit file reflects the improvements that the bureaus committed to implementing. The changes did not happen automatically for every affected consumer in every affected account. They happened imperfectly across a system that processes billions of data points monthly and makes errors at a rate that is invisible at the aggregate level but consequential at the individual level. Your file may contain medical entries that should have been removed a year ago and have not been because no one looked, no one disputed, and the automated systems that were supposed to catch them missed them. Looking now, disputing what should not be there, and using Claude to build the specific argument for each entry is the action that converts a policy change that sounds good into a credit file improvement that actually shows up in your score.

25

The Trump Credit Environment, Fintech Predators, and How to Use Claude to Identify a Predatory Loan Before You Sign Anything

The deregulation that opened doors for financial technology companies also opened doors for interest rates that would have been illegal five years ago. Here is how to tell the difference before the money lands in your account.

The financial technology lending landscape that exists in 2026 is the direct result of a deliberate regulatory shift that began with the current administration's executive order instructing federal regulators to remove barriers for non-bank fintech firms seeking national bank charters. The practical effect of that order is that companies which are not traditional banks and were never subject to traditional banking oversight can now access the national bank charter framework, which historically preempts state usury laws. State usury laws are the interest rate caps that individual states impose to protect their residents from predatory lending. When a lender obtains a national bank charter or partners with a nationally chartered bank through what the industry calls a rent-a-bank arrangement, those state interest rate caps no longer apply to that lender's products. The result is that loans carrying annual percentage rates of 100 percent, 150 percent, and in some documented cases above 300 percent are being offered to consumers in states that would have prohibited those rates entirely under pre-deregulation rules.

These products do not present themselves as predatory. They present themselves as accessible, fast, and flexible. The marketing language emphasizes approval speed, minimal documentation requirements, and availability to borrowers who have been turned down elsewhere. The target audience is explicitly people with damaged credit who are in a position of financial vulnerability and whose limited access to traditional credit makes the offer feel like an opportunity rather than a trap. A borrower who has spent two years rebuilding their credit after a bankruptcy is exactly the person this marketing is designed to reach, and understanding the mechanics of how these products work before encountering them is the protection that marketing is designed to prevent you from having.

The annual percentage rate is the single most important number in any lending decision and it is also the number that fintech marketing is most sophisticated at obscuring. An APR of 100 percent means that for every dollar you borrow, you will pay one dollar in interest over the course of a year. On a loan of two thousand dollars with a 12 month term at 100 percent APR, the total interest paid exceeds the original loan amount before the final payment is made. The monthly payment on that loan, which is the number the marketing typically emphasizes, sounds more manageable than the total cost stated plainly, which is exactly why the monthly payment is what gets featured in the advertisement and the APR is what gets buried in the fine print at the bottom of the application page.

The rent-a-bank structure that makes these rates legal under the current regulatory environment works through a partnership between the fintech company and a federally chartered bank that is located in a state with no usury cap or a very high one. The bank technically originates the loan, which means the bank's federal charter governs the interest rate rules rather than the borrower's state law. The fintech company then purchases the loan from the bank immediately after origination and services it going forward. The bank's involvement is largely administrative. The fintech company's involvement is commercial. The consumer's experience is entirely with the fintech company. But the legal structure of the transaction means that the fintech company can charge rates that its own state licensing would prohibit because the transaction is characterized as a bank loan rather than a fintech loan. Courts have evaluated this structure with mixed results and the regulatory agencies that might challenge it have reduced enforcement posture under the current administration, which means the structure is operating at scale in 2026 in a way that would have attracted significant regulatory scrutiny in prior years.

One piece of genuinely consumer-friendly legislation did emerge from the current administration's credit-related activity and it is worth knowing about because it addresses a specific and widely despised practice that has affected mortgage applicants for years. The trigger leads restriction signed into law on March 4, 2026, amends the FCRA to prohibit credit bureaus from selling consumer information to marketers based on a mortgage credit inquiry. Previously when you applied for a mortgage and a lender pulled your credit, the bureaus were permitted to sell your information to competing lenders within hours of the inquiry, resulting in the wave of unsolicited calls, emails, and mailers that mortgage applicants routinely experienced in the days following an application. The new law restricts this practice significantly, giving consumers meaningful protection from the information cascade that a mortgage application previously triggered. If you are preparing to apply for a mortgage, this protection now exists at the federal level and you do not need to opt out of anything for it to apply.

Claude is the analytical tool that closes the gap between a loan offer that sounds reasonable and one that actually is. Before signing any loan agreement, lending contract, or financing arrangement that is not from a traditional bank or credit union you have a prior relationship with, paste the loan terms into a Claude session and ask Claude to calculate the true APR, the total cost of the loan over its full term, the total interest paid as a dollar amount, and the effective monthly cost expressed as a percentage of the loan principal. Ask Claude to compare those numbers to what a credit union personal loan at current rates would cost for the same amount and term. Ask Claude whether the structure of the agreement contains any provisions that could increase the rate or extend the term under conditions described in the fine print. And ask Claude explicitly whether this loan structure resembles a rent-a-bank arrangement and what the implications of that structure are for your rights as a borrower in your state.

The answers Claude produces from that analysis are not legal advice and Claude will tell you that directly. What they are is a clear-eyed translation of the financial mathematics of the offer into terms that make the real cost visible before you commit to it. A borrower who sees that a two thousand dollar loan will cost four thousand two hundred dollars in total payments over eighteen months, compared to two thousand three hundred dollars for the same loan from a credit union, is in a fundamentally different position than a borrower who sees a monthly payment that looks affordable in isolation. The information was always in the loan documents. Claude makes it legible in the time it takes to paste a paragraph of terms into a chat window.

The broader credit environment that the current deregulatory posture has produced is one that rewards financial sophistication disproportionately. Borrowers who understand APR calculations, who recognize rent-a-bank structures, who know that their state usury protections may not apply to a nationally chartered lender, and who have access to alternatives like credit unions and community banks are navigating a different market than borrowers who do not have that knowledge. The purpose of this chapter is to compress that knowledge gap as much as possible in the space available, because the consumer who understands what they are looking at when a fintech lender offers them fast cash at a payment that sounds manageable is the consumer who is most likely to make a decision that serves their financial rebuild rather than reversing it. The credit repair you have done, the disputes you have sent, the positive payment history you have built, the score you have raised, all of that work is worth protecting from the first offer that arrives in your inbox after your score crosses a threshold that makes you visible to lenders who profit most from borrowers who are rebuilding and do not yet know exactly what they are being offered.

26

The Seven-Year Obsolescence Audit: How to Calculate Exactly When Every Negative Item on Your Credit Report Must Come Off and What to Do When It Does Not

The law built an expiration date into every negative mark on your credit report. Most people never check whether those dates have passed.

The seven-year reporting window is one of the most powerful consumer protections in the Fair Credit Reporting Act and one of the least used. Not because people do not know it exists. Most people who have spent any time researching credit repair have encountered the seven-year rule at some point. It is underused because knowing the rule exists and knowing how to apply it precisely to a specific account entry are two entirely different things, and the gap between those two levels of knowledge is where collectors and bureaus operate with the most impunity. A collector who reports a re-aged account is counting on the consumer not knowing the exact date the clock started. A bureau that continues to report an obsolete entry is counting on the consumer not doing the math. This chapter gives you the math and gives you Claude to run it.

The rule itself comes from 15 U.S.C. Section 1681c, which specifies the maximum period a consumer reporting agency may report various categories of negative information. For most negative items, the maximum reporting period is seven years. That category includes late payments, collections, charge-offs, repossessions, and most other derogatory marks that result from non-payment or default. The seven-year clock begins on a specific date that is defined precisely in the statute and that precision is exactly what makes this rule enforceable when you know how to apply it.

The date the clock starts is called the date of first delinquency. It is defined in the FCRA as the date of the commencement of the delinquency on the account that immediately preceded the action. In plain language that means the date you first missed a payment and never caught up on the path that eventually led to the negative status being reported. It is not the date the account was charged off. It is not the date the debt was sold to a collector. It is not the date of last activity. It is not the date the collection account was opened by the current collector. It is the date the original delinquency began, and everything else that happened afterward flows from that single date regardless of how many times the account changed hands or how many different collectors reported it over the years.

This distinction is the foundation of the re-aging violation and understanding it precisely is what makes the obsolescence audit work. Re-aging occurs when a collector or bureau reports a date of first delinquency that is more recent than the actual date the original delinquency began. The effect is that the seven-year clock appears to start later than it actually did, keeping the entry on your credit report longer than the law allows. Re-aging is prohibited under the FCRA and it is common enough that examining the date of first delinquency on every collection account and every charged-off account on your report should be a standard part of any credit review.

The obsolescence audit runs in a specific sequence. Start by identifying every negative account on your report, meaning every account that is not current and in good standing. For each negative account, locate the date of first delinquency as reported. This field appears on most bureau reports but it is sometimes labeled differently across bureaus. Equifax may show it as date of first delinquency. Experian may show it as first delinquency. TransUnion may show it as date of first delinquency or may include it within the account history narrative. If the field is not clearly labeled, look at the payment history grid and identify the first month where a late payment status appears without a return to current status afterward. That month is the approximate date of first delinquency and it is your starting point for the calculation.

Once you have the date of first delinquency for each account, the calculation is straightforward. Add seven years to that date. The result is the date by which the entry must be removed from your credit report under the FCRA. If that date has already passed and the entry is still on your report, the entry is obsolete and its continued presence is a violation of Section 1681c. If that date is approaching within the next six to twelve months, the entry will age off naturally and disputing it may or may not be worth your time depending on how much scoring weight it currently carries and whether other dispute priorities are more urgent.

Claude executes this calculation instantly and accurately when you give it the right inputs. Open a Claude session and paste every negative account entry from your credit report, including the date of first delinquency as reported for each one. Ask Claude to calculate the seven-year expiration date for every entry, identify which entries are already past their legal reporting window, identify which entries will age off within the next twelve months, and rank the remaining entries by how recently they were delinquent so you can prioritize your dispute campaign around the items causing the most active scoring damage. The output Claude produces is your obsolescence audit report and it takes a process that would require careful manual calculation for every account and compresses it into a single session.

For accounts that are past their seven-year window and still appearing on your report, the dispute is among the simplest in all of credit repair because the argument requires nothing more than the date. The entry is obsolete under 15 U.S.C. Section 1681c. The date of first delinquency as reported was the relevant date and seven years have passed. The bureau must remove it. There is no verification process that can save an obsolete entry because verifying the accuracy of the information reported does not change the fact that the reporting window has expired. Accuracy and timeliness are separate requirements under the FCRA and a bureau cannot satisfy the timeliness requirement by confirming the accuracy of the underlying information. Claude writes this dispute letter in a single prompt when you give it the account details and the calculated expiration date.

For accounts where re-aging is suspected, meaning accounts where the date of first delinquency as reported appears inconsistent with the age of the underlying debt, the dispute requires one additional layer of documentation. You need to establish what the actual date of first delinquency was, which means finding documentation that predates the reported date. A statement from the original creditor showing the first missed payment. A collection notice from an earlier collector that references an older date. A bankruptcy filing that listed the account with an earlier delinquency date. Any document that establishes the real origin date of the delinquency and contradicts the date the current furnisher is reporting creates the basis for a re-aging dispute that Claude can build into a specific and well-documented letter.

The accounts most likely to carry re-aged dates are older collection accounts that have been sold multiple times. Each sale creates an opportunity for the purchasing collector to enter a new date into their reporting system, either through error or through the deliberate practice of updating the date to extend the collectability of the account. Debts that are approaching the seven-year reporting window become significantly less valuable to collect because once they age off the credit report the collector loses the credit damage leverage that motivates many consumers to pay. Re-aging the account extends that leverage and some collectors exploit that incentive systematically. Claude identifies these accounts by looking for inconsistencies between the reported date of first delinquency and the age or history of the underlying debt as you describe it, and it flags the accounts most worth examining for re-aging violations based on the pattern of information you provide.

The obsolescence audit is not a one-time exercise. Run it when you first pull your reports and begin your dispute campaign. Run it again twelve months later to catch accounts that have newly crossed the seven-year threshold. Run it any time a new collection account appears on your report because the date of first delinquency on a newly reported collection should reflect the original delinquency date on the underlying debt, and a collector who opens a new trade line with a suspiciously recent date on an old debt is exhibiting exactly the re-aging pattern that the audit is designed to catch. The seven-year rule is a powerful consumer protection and it is most powerful in the hands of a consumer who knows exactly when it applies and what to do when it has been violated.

27

Special Purpose Credit Programs, the ECOA Regulation B Changes, and the Lending Pathways That Exist Outside Standard Credit Score Gatekeeping

There are lending programs designed specifically for people the standard system underserves. Most of the people who qualify for them have never heard of them.

The Equal Credit Opportunity Act has governed lending discrimination in the United States since 1974 and its implementing regulation, Regulation B, has shaped how lenders think about who qualifies for credit and on what terms for the same period. Most consumers know the ECOA only in its most basic form, which is the prohibition against denying credit based on race, color, religion, national origin, sex, marital status, age, or receipt of public assistance. What most consumers do not know is that the same law that prohibits discrimination also creates a specific carveout that allows lenders to design programs that affirmatively serve populations that standard underwriting systematically excludes. These programs are called Special Purpose Credit Programs and the regulatory changes that took effect in April and May of 2026 reshaped how they work in ways that create both new opportunities and new boundaries worth understanding precisely.

A Special Purpose Credit Program is a lending program operated by a for-profit institution, a nonprofit organization, or a government entity that is specifically designed to extend credit to a class of applicants who would not qualify under standard underwriting criteria. The purpose of the program is to serve a market that conventional lending overlooks, typically because the population being served lacks the credit history, the income documentation, or the collateral that standard approval algorithms require. Community development financial institutions have operated versions of these programs for decades. Banks operating in underserved communities have used them to satisfy Community Reinvestment Act obligations. Nonprofit housing organizations have used them to extend homeownership to first-generation buyers. What the 2026 Regulation B amendments did was clarify the conditions under which these programs can operate legally and specify the boundaries of what characteristics can and cannot be used to determine eligibility.

The practical implication of the 2026 amendments for a consumer rebuilding their credit is that Special Purpose Credit Programs represent a set of lending pathways that do not run through the standard FICO score gatekeeping that governs conventional lending. A borrower whose credit score is below the threshold for a conventional mortgage but who meets the eligibility criteria for a Special Purpose Credit Program operated by a community development lender may be able to access home financing that the conventional market would deny. A small business owner whose personal credit was damaged by pandemic-era financial disruption but whose business serves a community that qualifies for SPCP-backed lending may be able to access business capital that standard SBA lending criteria would exclude. The key is knowing these programs exist, knowing where to find them, and knowing which ones your specific situation qualifies you for.

The 2026 amendments eliminated what the regulatory framework called the effects test from the ECOA analysis for Special Purpose Credit Programs. The effects test previously required that any eligibility criteria used in an SPCP, even neutral-seeming criteria, be evaluated for whether they produced a disparate impact on protected classes. The elimination of that test does not mean lenders can now use eligibility criteria that directly discriminate. The amendments simultaneously established new explicit prohibitions on using race, color, national origin, or sex as the sole eligibility criteria for a for-profit SPCP. What the change does in practical terms is give lenders more flexibility in designing geographic, income-based, and community-focused eligibility criteria without the compliance burden of the effects test analysis, which had made some lenders reluctant to operate these programs at all. The net effect should be more programs in more markets serving more borrowers who fall outside standard underwriting parameters.

Finding Special Purpose Credit Programs that you qualify for requires knowing where to look because these programs are not marketed through the same channels as conventional lending products. Community development financial institutions, which are federally certified organizations specifically chartered to serve economically distressed communities, are the most consistent source of SPCP-adjacent lending. The CDFI Fund, which is administered by the Treasury Department, maintains a database of certified CDFIs searchable by state and lending type. A borrower in a qualifying geographic area who is seeking a small business loan, a mortgage, or a personal loan and whose credit profile falls below conventional thresholds should check the CDFI directory as a first step because CDFIs operate specifically to serve the population that conventional lenders decline.

Housing finance agencies operated by state governments are another source of programs that function similarly to SPCPs for mortgage lending purposes. Most states operate at least one housing finance agency that offers below-market interest rates, down payment assistance, and relaxed credit score requirements for first-time buyers or buyers in targeted communities. These programs are funded through tax-exempt bond programs and federal allocations and they are specifically designed to extend homeownership to borrowers who cannot access conventional financing. The credit score minimums for state housing finance agency programs are typically lower than conventional loan thresholds and some programs offer additional flexibility for borrowers with recent negative credit events including bankruptcy and foreclosure if sufficient time has passed and positive credit has been reestablished.

Claude is the research and analysis tool for navigating this landscape because the program availability, eligibility criteria, and geographic scope vary significantly across states, lenders, and program types and the information changes as programs open, close, and modify their terms. Give Claude your state of residence, your approximate credit score range, your income level, the type of financing you are seeking whether mortgage, small business, or personal, and any relevant characteristics of your situation such as whether you are a first-time homebuyer, whether your business operates in a low-income census tract, or whether you are a veteran or active military member. Ask Claude to identify the categories of Special Purpose Credit Programs and CDFI lending that your profile suggests you may qualify for and to describe the specific eligibility criteria and application process for each category. Claude cannot access real-time program databases but it can accurately map the landscape of program types, the organizations that typically operate them, and the eligibility frameworks that govern them, which gives you a specific research agenda to pursue rather than a general awareness that alternatives exist somewhere.

The broader point that Special Purpose Credit Programs represent in the context of this book is that the standard credit score gatekeeping system is not the only system. It is the dominant system and understanding how to optimize your position within it is the primary purpose of most of what this book covers. But for borrowers whose credit damage is recent enough that the conventional system remains inaccessible despite an active dispute and rebuild campaign, knowing that parallel pathways exist and knowing how to find and access them is the information that prevents a period of credit rebuilding from also being a period of complete financial stagnation. You can be actively repairing your credit file, actively building positive history, and actively pursuing financing through programs designed for exactly your situation simultaneously. Those three tracks run in parallel and the progress on each one accelerates the progress on the others. Claude helps you manage all three from a single planning conversation when you give it the full picture of where you are and where you are trying to go.

28

Negotiating With Creditors Directly: What to Say, How to Say It, When the Phone Call Is Worth Making, and When the Letter Is the Only Move That Protects You

Creditors negotiate every day. Most of them would rather settle than litigate. Knowing that changes the conversation entirely.

There is a version of credit repair that lives entirely in the dispute process, letters going to bureaus, responses coming back, deletions accumulating quietly over months of documented effort. That version works and this book has given you everything you need to execute it. But there is another track running parallel to the dispute process that most credit repair guides underemphasize because it requires a different skill set and a different mindset, and that is direct negotiation with the creditors and collectors who hold your accounts.

Negotiation works because the economics of debt collection are not what most consumers imagine them to be. A creditor who charged off your account years ago has already absorbed the accounting loss. They wrote the balance off their books. If the account was sold to a collector, the collector purchased it for a fraction of the face value, sometimes as little as three to seven cents on the dollar for older distressed debt. The collector's cost basis is not the balance they are pursuing. It is the small amount they paid to acquire the right to pursue it. That math creates room for negotiation that would not exist if the creditor were pursuing the full original value of what they lent.

The first principle of effective creditor negotiation is understanding what the other party actually needs from the conversation. A collector working a portfolio of distressed accounts needs to generate returns on that portfolio sufficient to cover their acquisition cost, their operating expenses, and a profit margin. An account that settles for forty cents on the dollar is a successful collection. An account that goes unresolved contributes nothing. A creditor weighing whether to pursue litigation on an old account is calculating whether the legal cost and time investment of a lawsuit is justified by the probability of a judgment and the subsequent probability of actually collecting on that judgment. For many old accounts the answer to that calculation is no, which means the creditor has less leverage than their collection notices suggest and more interest in settlement than their opening position implies.

The second principle is that everything that matters must be in writing. A phone conversation with a collector that results in a verbal agreement to settle for a reduced amount and delete the tradeline is worth nothing if the collector takes your payment and continues to report the account or sends it to a different collector. The agreement must be in writing, signed by an authorized representative of the collection company, and in your possession before a single dollar changes hands. This is not paranoia. It is the documented experience of thousands of consumers who settled verbally and discovered that verbal agreements with debt collectors are functionally unenforceable. The written agreement is the transaction. The payment is what follows the agreement, never what precedes it.

The third principle is that the opening offer is never the final position and your opening offer should reflect that reality. If a collector is pursuing a five thousand dollar balance and you have determined through your financial analysis that you can offer two thousand dollars as a lump sum settlement, your opening offer is not two thousand dollars. Your opening offer is twelve hundred dollars. You expect the collector to counter. You expect to move toward your actual number through two or three exchanges. Starting at your actual number leaves you nowhere to go when the counter comes and signals to the collector that your position is not as firm as it needs to be to produce the best settlement terms.

The written negotiation letter is often more effective than the phone call for a specific reason that has nothing to do with communication style and everything to do with legal protection. When you make a settlement offer in writing, you create a documented record of the offer, the terms you proposed, and the date you proposed them. If the collector accepts in writing, you have a binding agreement. If the collector ignores the letter or rejects it without a counter, you have documented evidence of your good faith attempt to resolve the account that becomes relevant if the situation ever escalates to litigation. The phone call produces none of that documentation and exposes you to the risk of a collector misrepresenting what was agreed or using information you share during the call in ways you did not anticipate.

Claude writes negotiation letters with the same precision it brings to dispute letters when you give it the account details, your proposed settlement amount, and the specific terms you are requesting. The terms that matter in a settlement letter are the settlement amount expressed as full and final satisfaction of the account, the deletion of the tradeline from all three credit bureaus rather than an update to paid or settled status, the timeframe for deletion after payment receipt, and the requirement that the agreement be signed by an authorized representative before payment is made. Ask Claude to write the letter incorporating all of those terms in formal business language that signals you understand your rights and the collector's legal obligations. That signal matters because collectors, like most negotiating parties, adjust their approach based on their assessment of how informed the person on the other side of the table is.

The accounts most worth pursuing through direct negotiation rather than pure dispute are accounts where the underlying debt is accurate but the balance or reporting contains errors, accounts where the debt is real and verifiable but old enough that the collector's leverage is diminishing as the seven-year reporting window approaches, and accounts where a settlement would produce a meaningful score improvement that the dispute process alone is unlikely to achieve quickly. Accurate negative information that is being reported correctly and within the legal reporting window is not removable through dispute but it may be negotiable if the creditor has sufficient incentive to settle and delete. Understanding which accounts fall into which category is the strategic analysis that Claude can help you complete before you decide whether to write a dispute letter, a negotiation letter, or both simultaneously.

The simultaneous approach is often the most effective for collection accounts specifically. A Section 611 dispute to the bureau and a Section 623 dispute to the collector run on the legal track while a settlement offer letter runs on the negotiation track at the same time. The legal pressure of the dispute creates urgency for the collector to resolve the account because a successful dispute that results in deletion is a worse outcome for the collector than a settlement that produces payment. The negotiation offer gives the collector a path to a better outcome than deletion without payment. The two tracks together create a situation where the collector's incentive is to accept the settlement, and many collectors do exactly that when both pressures are applied simultaneously and the settlement offer is reasonable relative to their cost basis on the account.

What you say if a collector calls you during this process is simpler than most people expect. You are not required to discuss the debt on the phone. You are not required to confirm your identity, your address, or any details about the account. You can tell the collector that all communication must be in writing and end the call. The FDCPA gives you the right to demand written communication and the collector must honor that demand. Once you have made it, every subsequent phone call from that collector is a potential FDCPA violation that adds to your legal leverage. Document the date and time of every call you receive after making the written communication demand. Those records become relevant if the harassment continues and you decide to file a CFPB complaint or consult a consumer law attorney about your options. The collector who calls repeatedly after a written communication demand is not just being aggressive. They are building your case for you.

29

Your 90-Day Credit Action Plan Built with Claude: The Exact Sequence of Steps, in the Exact Order, Starting From Wherever You Are Right Now

This is the chapter where reading stops and doing starts. Everything before this was preparation. This is the plan.

The gap between understanding credit repair and actually executing it is where most people stall. Not because the process is too complicated. Not because the law is too difficult to navigate. Because understanding a process and having a specific next action for tomorrow morning are two different things and most credit repair resources leave you with the former without giving you the latter. This chapter closes that gap. It gives you a 90 day sequence that starts from whatever your current situation is, runs through the dispute campaign, builds positive history simultaneously, and positions you at day 91 with measurable progress and a clear picture of what comes next.

Before the plan starts you need three things. Your credit reports from all three bureaus pulled from AnnualCreditReport.com within the last 30 days.

A Claude session open and ready to work. And a dedicated folder, physical or digital, where every document related to this process lives in one place. The folder is not optional. The paper trail you build over the next 90 days is the evidence base for every dispute, every escalation, and every legal argument that follows if anything goes wrong. People who lose disputes lose them because they cannot prove what they sent, when they sent it, and what response they received. The folder is the case file and the case file is the campaign.

Days one through seven are the audit and analysis phase. On day one you pull all three reports and read every entry. You make the list that chapter six described, every negative account, the creditor name, the account number, the reported balance, the date of first delinquency, and which bureaus are reporting it. On day two you open Claude and run the obsolescence audit from chapter twenty-six. You paste every negative entry and ask Claude to calculate the seven-year expiration date for each one, identify any entries that are already past the legal reporting window, and flag any dates of first delinquency that appear inconsistent with the age of the underlying debt. On day three you run the re-aging analysis for any accounts Claude flagged as potentially problematic. On day four you identify every medical entry on your reports and run it through the medical debt analysis from chapter twenty-four, checking balances against the sub-500 dollar exclusion threshold and payment status against the paid medical collection exclusion policy. On day five you complete the dispute priority ranking, ordering your accounts from the most legally vulnerable and highest scoring impact to the least, so your letters go out in the sequence that produces the fastest measurable improvement. On days six and seven you draft every dispute letter using Claude and the prompts throughout this book. You do not mail anything yet. You draft everything first so the entire campaign is ready to launch simultaneously.

Days eight through fourteen are the launch phase. On day eight you mail your first round of dispute letters. Every letter goes certified mail with return receipt requested. You record the tracking number for every letter in your folder alongside a copy of every letter you sent. You record the mailing date. You calculate the 30-day response deadline for each letter and write those deadlines in your folder as well. On day nine you send your debt validation letters to any collectors you are pursuing simultaneously with the bureau disputes. Same certified mail discipline. Same tracking number documentation. On day ten you send your Section 623 direct furnisher dispute letters to the original creditors or collectors where the dispute argument runs through the furnisher rather than just the bureau. By the end of day ten you have three parallel tracks running simultaneously, bureau disputes, debt validation demands, and furnisher disputes, all with documented send dates and calculable response deadlines.

Days eleven through thirty are the monitoring phase. Nothing significant happens in this window and that is correct. The bureaus and collectors are running their investigation timelines. Your job during this period is to do two things. First, open your secured credit card account if you have not already done so and execute the first month of your positive credit building campaign exactly as chapter fifteen described. One small recurring purchase. Full balance paid three to five days before the statement closing date. That is the entire instruction for month one of the build. Second, document anything that arrives in the mail related to your disputes. Every bureau response, every collector response, every debt validation response goes into your folder with the date received noted on the document. Do not respond to anything yet. Collect and document through day thirty.

Days thirty-one through forty-five are the response analysis phase. By day thirty most of your dispute letters should have generated responses. Read every response carefully and categorize each one. A deletion or correction confirmed in writing is a win. Document it, verify it appears correctly on your updated report when you pull it, and move to the next item. A verified response, meaning the bureau investigated and determined the item is accurate, is not the end. It is the beginning of the escalation track.

Document the verified response, the date you received it, and what the bureau claims it verified. A non-response, meaning no response arrived within the 30 day window, is a potential FCRA violation. Document the mailing date, the certified mail delivery confirmation date, and the 30-day deadline that passed without a response. Non-responses and verified responses both generate the next round of letters, which Claude helps you write based on the specific response you received.

Days forty-six through sixty are the escalation phase. Every non-response gets a CFPB complaint filed on day forty-six. Every verified response that you believe was not the result of a genuine investigation gets a method of verification request letter under Section 1681i. Every collector who failed to validate a debt and continued collection activity gets a formal FDCPA violation notice. Every furnisher who failed to respond to your Section 623 direct dispute gets a follow-up letter citing Regulation V and the 30-day deadline that passed. This is also the phase where you assess your settlement negotiation opportunities. For accounts where the dispute outcome looks uncertain and a settlement would produce a better result than continued dispute, day forty-six is when the settlement offer letters go out alongside the escalation letters on the legal track.

Days sixty-one through ninety are the consolidation and build phase. The dispute campaign is largely complete by this point. Some items will have been deleted. Some will be in the escalation process. Some will require attorney consultation if the bureau and furnisher responses suggest a pattern of noncompliance that goes beyond what the consumer dispute process can address. Your attention shifts in this phase toward the credit building side. By day sixty you should have two months of clean payment history on your secured card. Now you evaluate whether a credit builder loan is the right next step based on your current account mix and the progress your score has shown. You pull your reports again at day seventy-five to verify that deletions have been correctly applied, that no deleted items have reappeared, and that no new inaccurate entries have appeared since your initial audit.

You document what you find.

On day ninety you do a full assessment. Pull all three reports. Run Claude through the updated entries and ask Claude to compare your current file to the starting point you documented on day one. Ask Claude to calculate the approximate score impact of every deletion that was achieved, identify what remains to be addressed in the next campaign cycle, and build you the next 90-day plan from your new starting point. The first 90 days are not the end of the process. They are the proof of concept that the process works and the foundation for the next phase, which is faster and lighter because the heaviest disputes are behind you and the positive history you built in the first three months is already compounding forward.

Claude sits at the center of every phase of this plan not as a replacement for your own judgment and your own actions but as the analytical and drafting engine that makes the judgment easier to apply and the actions faster to execute. Give Claude your audit results and it builds your dispute priority list. Give Claude your dispute reason and account details and it writes the letter. Give Claude the bureau's response and it tells you whether the response satisfies the legal standard or gives you grounds for escalation. Give Claude your 90-day progress report and it builds the next plan. The work is yours. The tools are here. The law is on your side. Day one starts whenever you decide it does.

30

Using Claude Beyond Credit Repair: Advanced Prompts for Budgeting, Loan Analysis, Business Planning, and Building the Financial Life That Credit Was Always Supposed to Support

The same tool that helped you dispute a collection account can help you negotiate a salary, analyze a business loan, and build a financial plan that does not depend on debt to function.

Most people who come to Claude for credit repair discover something unexpected partway through the process. The tool that reads their credit report entries and writes their dispute letters is the same tool that can read a loan agreement and tell them whether the terms are predatory, read a job offer and tell them whether the salary is competitive for their market, read a lease and tell them what the landlord can and cannot legally do, and read their monthly expenses and tell them where the money is actually going versus where they think it is going. Claude is a reasoning tool and the reasoning it applies to a Section 611 dispute letter is the same reasoning it applies to any document, any set of numbers, or any decision that benefits from careful analysis of the specific facts at hand.

This chapter is about expanding your use of Claude beyond the credit repair campaign that brought you here. Not because the credit repair work is less important but because the financial life you are building toward requires more than a clean credit file. It requires income that exceeds expenses consistently. It requires the ability to evaluate financial products before committing to them. It requires a business framework if entrepreneurship is part of your plan. It requires the kind of ongoing financial analysis that used to require either an expensive professional or an unusual amount of personal expertise to access. Claude makes that analysis available to anyone who knows how to ask for it and this chapter gives you the prompts.

The budgeting application is the most immediate and the most underutilized. Most people who struggle with cash flow management have tried budgeting in some form and found the traditional approach unsustainable because it requires continuous attention and produces guilt rather than clarity when the tracking reveals spending patterns that do not match the intended budget. Claude approaches budgeting differently when you give it the right prompt. Instead of tracking what you spent, you give Claude what you earn and what you owe and ask it to design a cash flow allocation system that funds your obligations automatically before discretionary spending begins. The prompt that works is specific. Tell Claude your monthly take-home income after taxes. Tell Claude every fixed monthly obligation, the amount and the due date. Tell Claude your variable monthly necessities, food, transportation, and personal care with your best estimate of what each costs. Ask Claude to design an allocation sequence that covers every fixed obligation, funds a specific savings amount you designate, covers your variable necessities, and leaves a clear discretionary amount that you can spend without tracking because everything that matters was funded first. Ask Claude to identify which obligations fall on which dates and flag any cash flow gaps where obligations cluster in a way that creates timing risk even when the monthly total is manageable.

The loan analysis application is one of the most valuable uses of Claude for someone whose credit recovery has progressed to the point where lenders are making offers. Any loan offer, whether a personal loan, an auto loan, a mortgage, a business line of credit, or a credit card with a balance transfer offer, can be analyzed by Claude in the time it takes to paste the key terms into a chat window. The prompt that produces the most useful analysis asks Claude to calculate the true annual percentage rate if it is not clearly stated, the total cost of the loan over its full term expressed as a dollar amount rather than a percentage, the total interest paid as a ratio of the original loan amount, the monthly payment and how it fits within your current cash flow allocation, and a comparison of those numbers to what the same loan would cost from a credit union or community bank at current market rates. Ask Claude to flag any terms in the agreement that could change the rate or extend the term under conditions described in the fine print, including variable rate provisions, prepayment penalties, and automatic renewal clauses. The analysis Claude produces from those inputs is not legal advice and Claude will tell you that directly, but it is an accurate translation of the financial mathematics of the offer into terms that make the real cost visible before you commit.

The salary and income negotiation application is one that most people never think to bring to Claude and it is genuinely useful. When you receive a job offer or are preparing for a salary review, give Claude the offered salary, your current salary if applicable, your years of experience, your geographic market, your industry, and the specific role title. Ask Claude to assess whether the offered compensation is competitive for your market and experience level based on publicly available compensation data. Ask Claude to draft a counteroffer response that makes the case for a higher number based on your specific qualifications and the market data rather than on your personal need for more money. Salary negotiation framed around market data and demonstrated value produces better outcomes than negotiation framed around personal circumstances and Claude helps you construct the market-based argument in writing before you make it verbally. A written counteroffer also creates a record that protects you if the verbal conversation diverges from what was agreed.

The business planning application is relevant for anyone who is building a business alongside their credit recovery, which is a common situation because entrepreneurship and financial disruption often coincide and the skills that drive someone to rebuild their credit are often the same skills that drive them to build something. Give Claude your business concept, your target market, your estimated startup costs, your projected monthly revenue in the first year based on your most conservative estimate, and your projected monthly expenses. Ask Claude to assess whether the business model is financially viable at your projected revenue level, identify the specific revenue threshold at which the business covers its expenses and pays you a sustainable income, calculate how long it will take to reach that threshold at your projected growth rate, and identify the three or four variables in your projections that have the most impact on the outcome so you know where to focus your attention and your uncertainty. Ask Claude to identify the financing options most likely to be available to a business at your stage given your personal credit situation and the business credit profile you are building. The output is not a business plan in the formal sense but it is the financial analysis that a business plan needs to be built on and it is available in a single Claude session when you give it the right inputs.

The contract and agreement review application applies to any written agreement you are asked to sign that has financial consequences. A commercial lease for business space. A vendor agreement with payment terms. A partnership agreement with profit sharing provisions. A contractor agreement with liability clauses. A subscription service with automatic renewal and cancellation terms. Paste the relevant sections into Claude and ask Claude to identify every provision that creates a financial obligation, every provision that could change the terms under conditions described in the document, every provision that limits your rights or creates liability, and every term that appears unusual relative to standard practice in that type of agreement. Claude is not a lawyer and will tell you that when the analysis warrants it, but Claude reads documents with a thoroughness that most people do not apply when reviewing agreements under the social pressure of a signing situation, and the provisions that create the most problems are almost always the ones that seemed like boilerplate at signing.

The financial goal planning application ties everything together. Once your credit repair campaign is underway, your cash flow is structured, and your positive credit building is in motion, give Claude the full picture of where you are and where you want to go. Your current income. Your current net worth including assets and liabilities. Your credit profile in general terms. Your three to five year financial goals, whether that is homeownership, business ownership, a specific savings target, retirement contribution, or debt freedom. Ask Claude to build a sequenced financial plan that addresses each goal in the order that makes the most mathematical sense given your current position, identifies the specific milestones that mark progress toward each goal, and flags the financial decisions that would most significantly accelerate or delay your progress depending on how you handle them. The plan Claude builds is specific to your numbers and your goals in a way that generic financial advice cannot be, and it gives you a document to return to as your situation evolves and your goals become more defined.

The common thread across all of these applications is that Claude does its best work when you give it specific inputs rather than general questions. A general question produces a general answer. A specific question with real numbers, real terms, and real context produces analysis that is actually useful for the decision you are trying to make. The credit repair prompts throughout this book are long and structured because that structure is what makes the output specific and actionable. The same principle applies to every other financial application. Give Claude the real numbers. Give Claude the actual document. Give Claude the specific decision you are facing. The reasoning it brings to your situation is the same reasoning it brings to every situation and it is available to you at any hour, for any question, at whatever pace your financial life requires.

31

How to Monitor Your Credit After the Repair Is Done: What to Watch, When to Pull Your Reports, and How to Protect What Took You Months to Build

The campaign is over. The work is not. Here is what ongoing credit health actually looks like in practice.

There is a specific kind of financial vulnerability that arrives after a successful credit repair campaign and it is worth naming directly because almost nobody talks about it. You spent months disputing, building, monitoring, and managing. The score moved. The deletions happened. The positive history accumulated. And then the urgency that drove all of that discipline quietly fades because the emergency is over and the habits that the emergency enforced no longer have the same pressure behind them. The credit file that took months to clean can accumulate new damage much faster than it accumulated the damage you just removed, and the monitoring discipline that protected your progress during the active campaign is the same discipline that needs to continue after it, just with less intensity and more automation.

The foundation of post-repair credit monitoring is knowing what your file looks like when it is healthy so that you recognize immediately when something changes. Pull all three reports the week after your campaign produces its final resolved outcomes. Read every entry. Note every account that is reporting and in what status. Note your utilization across every revolving account. Note your oldest account and your average account age. Note the absence of any derogatory marks that were deleted during the campaign. That snapshot is your baseline and it is the document you compare against every subsequent report pull to identify changes that require attention.

How often you pull your reports after the campaign depends on where you are in your financial life. If you are actively preparing for a major credit application like a mortgage or a business loan, pull all three reports every thirty to forty-five days and review every entry with the same thoroughness you applied during the campaign. Changes to your file in the months before a major application can affect your qualifying score in ways that are difficult to correct quickly if you discover them close to the application date. If you are in a maintenance phase with no major application on the immediate horizon, pulling your reports every three to four months is sufficient for most people. AnnualCreditReport.com provides one free report from each bureau per year under the standard federal entitlement, and since 2020 the bureaus have offered free weekly reports through the same portal, which means there is no cost barrier to pulling your reports as frequently as your situation warrants.

The specific things to look for when you review your reports in the post-campaign period fall into four categories. The first is re-insertion, which is when a deleted item reappears on your report after having been removed. Re-insertion is prohibited under the FCRA without specific conditions being met, including prior written notice to you, but it happens and it happens often enough that checking for it should be a standard part of every post-campaign report review. If a deleted item reappears without the required notice, that is a separate FCRA violation from the original reporting error and it generates a new dispute with additional legal weight behind it. Claude writes the re-insertion dispute letter when you give it the deletion date, the date the item reappeared, and the account details, and the argument is straightforward because the FCRA's re-insertion rules are specific and unambiguous.

The second category is new inaccurate entries, which can arrive at any time through data errors, identity confusion, or the normal imperfection of a system that processes billions of account updates monthly. A new entry that appears on your report from a creditor you do not recognize, an inquiry from a company you never applied to, or an account status change that does not reflect your actual payment history all warrant immediate investigation and dispute if the entry is inaccurate. The post-campaign consumer is better equipped to identify and address these quickly because the dispute process is no longer new and the Claude prompts that build the letters are familiar tools rather than a learning curve.

The third category is identity theft indicators, which are among the most urgent issues to catch early because the damage from undetected identity theft compounds faster than almost any other credit problem. A new account you did not open, an address on your file that is not yours or has never been yours, an employer listed that you have never worked for, hard inquiries from lenders you never contacted, these are the signals that someone else is using your credit file to obtain financing. The moment you see any of these indicators, freeze your credit at all three bureaus immediately. A credit freeze is free under federal law and it prevents any new account from being opened in your name until you lift it. File an identity theft report with the FTC at identitytheft.gov. Contact each creditor where fraudulent accounts were opened. And use the Section 1681c-2 dispute process covered in the identity theft chapter to block the fraudulent entries from your report within the expedited four business day window that the FCRA provides for documented identity theft cases.

The fourth category is utilization creep, which is the gradual accumulation of revolving balances that happens when the discipline of the active campaign period relaxes and credit cards that were paid to zero during the rebuild phase start carrying balances again. Utilization creep is not an inaccuracy and it is not disputable. It is a behavioral pattern that produces a real and measurable score decline that only reverses when the balances are paid down again. Catching it early through regular report monitoring means catching it when the balances are small and the paydown is manageable rather than catching it when the pattern has run for a year and the score has dropped significantly. Set a personal utilization threshold, ten to fifteen percent of total available revolving credit is the target range that maximizes scoring benefit, and treat any report pull that shows aggregate utilization above that threshold as an action item for the current billing cycle rather than something to address later.

Credit monitoring services offer an automated version of the report review process and they are worth evaluating as a supplement to your own periodic reviews. The free monitoring services offered by many credit card issuers and personal finance apps provide score tracking and alert notifications when significant changes occur in your file, including new accounts, new inquiries, derogatory mark additions, and address changes. These alerts do not replace the full report review but they function as an early warning system that catches changes between your scheduled full reviews and gives you the opportunity to investigate and respond before the change has time to compound. The paid monitoring services that offer three-bureau monitoring and identity theft insurance are worth considering for consumers who have experienced identity theft previously or who are in active preparation for a major credit application where unexpected changes would be most costly.

Claude remains useful in the monitoring phase even after the active dispute campaign is complete. When your periodic report review surfaces something that needs attention, bring it to Claude the same way you brought your initial dispute items. Paste the entry, describe what changed and when, and ask Claude to assess whether the change represents an inaccuracy, a re-insertion, an identity theft indicator, or an accurate update that reflects something that actually happened in your account. Ask Claude to write the appropriate response letter if one is warranted. The tool that helped you build the clean file is the same tool that helps you protect it and the prompts that worked during the campaign work just as well in the maintenance phase because the underlying process is the same. Something appeared on your report. You assess whether it belongs there. If it does not, you dispute it. If it does, you address the behavior that produced it. That cycle runs for as long as you have a credit file, which is for as long as you are a participant in the financial system, and Claude makes every iteration of that cycle faster and more precise than it would be without it.

The credit file you have built is not fragile. It is the product of documented legal effort, consistent positive behavior, and a systematic approach to the rules that govern consumer credit reporting. Those are durable foundations and they do not unravel quickly when something goes wrong as long as you catch the problem early and respond with the same systematic approach that built the file in the first place. The monitoring practice described in this chapter is the maintenance layer that keeps the foundation intact. It takes less time than the campaign took. It requires less effort than the rebuild required. And it protects an asset that took months to construct from the kinds of damage that take much less time to inflict than to repair.

32

Your Credit Is a File, Not a Verdict: What Comes After the Letters, After the Score, and After the System No Longer Has a Hold on You

This is not the end of the story. It is the first chapter of a different one.

There is a moment that happens somewhere in the credit repair process that nobody warns you about because it is not dramatic enough to make it into the marketing materials and it is not painful enough to make it into the cautionary narratives. It is quiet and it arrives unexpectedly. You pull your credit report and the thing that used to be there is gone. The collection account that has been sitting on your file for four years, the one you saw every time you checked your score and felt the specific kind of helplessness that comes from knowing something is costing you and not being able to stop it, is simply not there anymore. The bureau investigated. The entry could not be verified. The law required deletion and deletion happened. The file looks different than it did before you started.

That moment is worth sitting with for a minute before you move to the next item on the list.

Not because the work is finished. It is not. But because the proof of concept that most people need before they truly believe the process works is that first deletion, that first letter that produced a result, that first confirmation that the system which seemed designed to be immovable has a mechanism built into it that moves when you push it correctly. The FCRA is not perfect. The dispute process is not fast. The bureaus are not on your side. But the law is real, the rights it grants are enforceable, and the tools in this book and in the Federal 609 application give you access to those rights in a form that does not require a law degree or a monthly credit repair subscription to use.

Credit repair is ultimately an act of self-advocacy and self-advocacy requires a specific kind of belief that most people who have been through financial hardship have had systematically eroded. The belief that you have standing. That your position matters. That the documentation you gathered and the letter you sent and the certified mail receipt you kept are the foundation of a legal argument that the bureau is required by federal law to take seriously. That belief is not naive. It is accurate. The FCRA gives every American consumer the right to dispute inaccurate information in their credit file, the right to demand that unverifiable information be deleted, the right to request the method by which a dispute was investigated, and the right to seek damages when those rights are violated. Those are not suggestions. They are statutes. They have been tested in federal court. They stand.

What comes after the repair is something this book has tried to point toward throughout its chapters but that ultimately only becomes real through the living of it. A credit score above 700 does not feel the way people expect it to feel. It does not announce itself. It does not produce a sudden sense of financial security or a flood of opportunities presenting themselves simultaneously. What it does is quietly remove friction from decisions that previously required extraordinary effort or were simply unavailable. The apartment application that gets approved without a co-signer. The auto loan that comes back at a rate that reflects your actual risk profile rather than penalizing you for a history you spent months correcting. The mortgage pre-approval that makes a conversation about homeownership real rather than theoretical. These are not dramatic moments. They are ordinary financial transactions that most people take for granted and that feel like something completely different when they were previously out of reach.

The financial life that becomes available after credit repair is not defined by what your score allows you to borrow. It is defined by what you choose to do with access that you rebuilt deliberately and understand deeply. Someone who went through the dispute process, who sent the certified mail, who tracked the deadlines, who escalated when the bureau failed to respond, who built the positive history account by account and month by month, understands the credit system in a way that most people who have always had good credit do not. They understand what the entries mean and where they come from. They understand what the law requires and what recourse exists when the law is violated. They understand that the score is an output and that the inputs are within their control. That understanding is not something the score itself conveys. It is earned through the process of repairing it and it is more durable than any number on a report.

The pandemic left financial damage across the country at a scale that the statistics capture but that the individual experience of living through it makes much more personal and much more varied than any aggregate number suggests. Lost income. Accumulated debt. Missed payments during periods when keeping a roof overhead required every available dollar. Small businesses that did not survive. Households that are still carrying the credit consequences of decisions that were not failures of character or discipline but responses to conditions that were genuinely extraordinary. If that description fits your situation, the core message of this book is not that the system will treat you fairly if you navigate it correctly. The system has significant structural problems that a dispute letter cannot fix. The message is that within the system as it exists, you have more rights and more tools and more leverage than the industry that profits from your confusion wants you to know about, and using those rights, those tools, and that leverage is available to you regardless of how the damage happened or how long it has been sitting on your file.

Claude is not a credit repair service. Federal 609 is not a credit repair service. This book is not a credit repair service. They are tools and knowledge and access, and the distinction matters because a credit repair service positions itself between you and your rights, charging a fee to exercise on your behalf the rights that the law already gave you directly. What this project has tried to do from the first book through this one through the platform is collapse that distance. Put the statute citations in your hands. Put the letter templates in your hands. Put the AI reasoning capacity in your hands. Put the platform that generates the letters in your hands. And then trust you to handle the rest, which the people who have used these tools have demonstrated they can do, consistently, at a fraction of the cost that the credit repair industry charges for the same access.

The credit file is a document. It contains data. Data can be wrong and when it is wrong the law gives you a mechanism to correct it. Data ages and when it ages past the legal reporting window the law requires its removal. Data can be unverifiable and when it cannot be verified the law requires deletion. None of those mechanisms are secret. None of them require professional intermediation. All of them require that you know they exist, that you understand how to invoke them, and that you have the tools to execute the process correctly. This book was written to give you all three.

Whatever brought you here, whether you are starting a dispute campaign tomorrow or finishing one that is mostly complete or somewhere in the middle of a process that has taken longer than you expected and produced results that are slower than you hoped, the work you are doing is worth doing. Not because a credit score is the most important thing in a financial life. It is not. But because the friction that damaged credit creates touches almost every financial decision you try to make and removing that friction opens up energy and attention and resources that were previously absorbed by the cost of navigating a system that was penalizing you for a past that does not have to define your future.

The letters you send are the beginning. The score that moves is the evidence. The financial life you build from there is the point.

Go to federal609.com. Get your first letter free. Send it certified. Keep the tracking number.

The clock starts when it arrives.

federal609.com

Fix Your Credit. Know the Law.

33

APPENDIX: MORE FROM POP BUCHANAN

Pop Buchanan is a New York City native, author, podcaster, speaker, and recovery educator with over thirteen years of sobriety. He holds a Bachelor of Science in Business from SUNY Farmingdale and has built one of the most diverse independent publishing catalogs in the self-help and personal finance space. His work spans addiction recovery, nervous system healing, artificial intelligence investment research, and consumer financial empowerment. Everything he writes comes from lived experience first and research second. That combination is what makes the catalog worth exploring beyond whichever book brought you here.

All titles are available at soberisdopebooks.com.

If you want to understand your credit repair options more deeply**, the companion to this book is Credit Repair 2026 with ChatGPT: Fix Your Credit Fast with a Step-by-Step Law-Based System Using AI, Legal 609 and 611 Disputes, Trump-Era Reporting Changes, and the New 2026 Credit Rules. That book is where the full legal framework lives. It covers how the bureaus work, how to pull your reports, the complete dispute method, medical debt, student loans, SBA reporting, and the ChatGPT-specific workflow for rebuilding your credit from the ground up. If you read this book first, go back to that one. If you read that one first, you already know why you picked this one up. Both books work together and neither replaces the other.

If you are interested in where artificial intelligence, quantum computing, and the next generation of technology investment are heading, the InvestAI Series is Pop Buchanan's research-driven book series examining long-cycle technological transformation and what it means for investors, entrepreneurs, and anyone trying to understand the economic forces shaping the next several decades. The series currently includes six titles. Invest AI: The Last Gold Rush in AI Stock Investments is Book 1 and the entry point for the series. Invest AI Quantum: Top Quantum Computing, Machine Learning, and AI Companies Shaping the Future of Investing is Book 2. Invest AI Robotics: How Artificial Intelligence, Quantum Computing, Robotics, and Blockchain Are Building the Next 40 Years of Stock Investments, DePIN Systems, and Native Crypto Economies is Book 3. Invest AI Crypto: The Investor's Guide to Artificial Intelligence, Machine Learning, Quantum Computing, and the Top Cryptocurrency Blockchains from Bitcoin to Solana to Bittensor and DePIN Networks is Book 4. Invest AI Quantum Computing Stacks: Top Quantum Computing Stack Companies Shaping the Future of AI and Long-Term Investments is Book 5. Invest AI Inference Chips: How NVIDIA, Amazon, Tesla, SpaceX, and AI Giants Are Racing to Control Hardware, Power, and Scale is Book 6. The InvestAI series does not offer trading tips or market predictions. It studies technological inevitability at the systems level and gives readers the intellectual framework to understand what is happening before the mainstream conversation catches up to it.

If you or someone you love is navigating addiction recovery, the Sober Is Dope library is where Pop Buchanan's most personal work lives. The Sober Is Dope Series currently includes two core titles. Sober Is Dope: Sobriety Prayers and Affirmations for Attracting Health, Happiness, and Abundance in Recovery is the foundational book, packed with 365 daily affirmations, 20 healing prayers, a 15-day devotional, and practical tools for early recovery grounded in faith, neuroscience, and lived experience. Sober Is Dope: Protect Your Sobriety: Why Relapse Happens and How the Brain and Nervous System Heal is the second title, written for anyone who wants to understand why relapse builds long before a craving appears and how the nervous system heals after substances are removed. Beyond those two titles, the Sober Healing Series covers nervous system regulation and vagus nerve activation. The Weed and Brain Reset Series addresses marijuana dependence and the neuroscience of quitting. The Manifestation Field Series bridges spiritual practice and behavioral science. The Sober Is Dope Podcast, one of the top recovery podcasts in its category with over 350 episodes, extends the conversation beyond the books.

If you follow sports and want data-driven intelligence for MLB, NFL, and NBA, POPR Sports Lab is the analytical platform built by POPR Technologies that brings the same systematic thinking behind Federal 609 to sports intelligence. The platform is live at poprsportslab.com and runs three modules. The MLB intelligence module covers home run targets, pitcher matchups, team stacks, curated player rankings with tier classifications, and an engine integrity system that flags analytical inconsistencies in real time. The NFL intelligence module covers game totals, defensive weakness identification, and weekly signal summaries across the full slate. The NBA intelligence module launched in Phase 1 for the 2025-26 season with live game intelligence activating for the 2026-27 season. System online. Data live. Go to poprsportslab.com.

If you are an entrepreneur, a builder, or someone with an idea you want to bring to life**, POPR Technologies is the technology arm of this ecosystem. POPR builds tools that convert published knowledge into deployable products, starting with Federal 609, the credit dispute letter platform that accompanies this book. If you are interested in what POPR is building or want to explore a partnership, the starting point is federal609.com.

For AI tools, creative technology, and anything that lives at the intersection of artificial intelligence and invention, visit poprtech.com.

The full publishing catalog across all series and imprints is at soberisdopebooks.com. The companion app to this book is at federal609.com. Scan the QR code at the back of this book to go directly to your free Section 609 letter.

www.ingramcontent.com/pod-product-compliance
Lightning Source LLC
LaVergne TN
LVHW090406210926
848480LV00002B/473

* 9 7 9 8 2 5 6 1 1 3 1 2 4 *